Vikram Seth's
A Suitable Boy
Search for an Indian Identity

In the same series

Indian Literature Today
R.K. Dhawan, ed.

Recent Indian Fiction
R.S. Pathak, ed.

Fiction of the Nineties
R.K. Dhawan and Veena Noble Dass, ed.

Feminism and Literature
Veena Noble Dass, ed.

Vikram Seth's
A Suitable Boy
Search for an Indian Identity

Shyam S. Agarwalla

PRESTIGE

Published by
Prestige Books
New Delhi 110 008

1995
Reprint 1998

ISBN: 81-85218-97-8

Photo Typesetting by
Pivot Computers
Delhi 110 006
Ph. 2934490

Printed at
Mehra Offset Press
New Delhi 110 002

Contents

Preface
7

A Suitable Boy:
Vikram Seth's Magnum Opus
9

**Critical Response to *A Suitable Boy*:
A Scrutiny**
25

**Something is Rotten . . .:
A Political Analysis of *A Suitable Boy***
31

**The Chatterjees and Cuddles:
Metaphor and Image in *A Suitable Boy***
49

The Multiple Plot in *A Suitable Boy*
62

Yinglish in *A Suitable Boy*
72

**The Tajmahal and the Victoria Memorial:
The Novels of Salman Rushdie and Vikram Seth**
87

Bibliography
94

Index
96

Preface

Empty tea cups pile up, the mortal body tires, the family accuses. The hands holding *A Suitable Boy* (1349 pages) tire as weight is transferred left to right, page by page, line by line, word by word. So much has already been read, and yet so much still remains. Gone are the days of youth when a *Martin Chuzzlewit* or *Middlemarch* or *Mahabharata* (twelve volumes) acted as valium for an agile and insomniac mind. No electronic gadgets, like the Zee TV were there to rob me of an ennui which, in my case, was a disease.

Then, the hectic and tormentic pace of the life of a principal and social worker, in the middle age, has robbed me of a half-lit literary activity. Suddenly, *A Suitable Boy* landed in my lap as a heaven-sent boon. At first, the elephantine size, the page monstering, and, what is more, the forbidding price, of the novel, frightened me as if I, like Horatio or Marcellus, have seen the ghost of Vikram Seth, at noon. But the veil of fright lifted, slowly, as I went on reading the novel. Suspense superseded curiosity, characters raised the antenna of knowledge, and language improved my knowledge of India. Indubitably, Vikram Seth is a master story-teller.

But, one question nagged me, like the nagging of a half-literate and good-natured wife. Is length and its lack represent essentially different views of what a novel should be? Supporters of the short novels of R.K. Narayan, Bharati Mukherjee, Upamanyu Chatterjee and Partap Sharma might say, with complacency, that the world is finite and containable within art. Supporters of the long novels of Charles Dickens, Leo Tolstoy, Henry James and Vikram Seth maintain the exact opposite. We fall between two stools.

Lawrence Norfolk answers: "Long, complex novels demand high levels of technical ability on the part of both writers and readers, but there is no evidence of any shortage in either camp. I do not know if the small little production numbers and attractively packaged chaff periodically trotted out with their surgical-strike marketing campaigns . . . represent a decline in literary standards. But they are certainly missed chances. Reality is not smart, or little, or attractively packaged, and never has been. Almost alone among the arts, the novel retains the formal capacity to treat of a subject in detail and at length, which is to say that it's upto the task. It needs to be remembered that now. Today, as before, it needs to be big. "My book has grown out of conviction that pagemonsters are not always taxing, and they must not and ought not frighten a busy scholar and teacher.

Then, to find out a suitable title for my critical study of *A Suitable Boy* proved to be as time-consuming and difficult as the search of a suitable boy for a suitable girl, in the Dunkel-infected India. Nayantara Sahgal quizzes on her identity (and, that of every Indian) in "Some Thoughts on the Puzzle of Identity" in her Arthur Ravenscroft Memorial Lecture, delivered at the University of Leeds, 18 February 1993. On the contrary, Upamanyu Chatterjee puzzles us in *English, August*. Salahuddin Pervez, in his Sahitya Akademi winning Urdu novel *Identity Card* (1989) and in his powerful blank verse writes: "I have merged the Kurukshetra of my heart/With the Kurukshetra of my mind/And declared/I want to battle." In this vigorous and intellectual search for an Indian identity, in the eighties and nineties, Vikram Seth, in *A Suitable Boy,* provides a suitable resting-place for the tired nerves and souls of our intellectuals. I, therefore, have chosen a title for my book: *Vikram Seth's "A Suitable Boy": Search for an Indian Identity*. If you disagree vehemently with my critical study of the novel or its title or both I shall be pleased. We arrive at values through dialectic. 'Vadé Vadé Jayate Tatva Bodha.'

I have a duty to acknowledge my indebtedness to my teachers, Dr. Tension and Mr. Patience whose gentle goading led to my writing. I owe a sense of gratitude to Prof. S. Ballabh for his valuable suggestions. I owe a sense of humility to my suitable wife, Satyabhama, to my obedient sons and daughters, Lalit, Pawan, Sunita and Sangita. Can I forget the grandfatherly love bestowed on me by Nidhi, Sweetie, Neha, Yukti and Aditya ?

Mercifully, God has chosen a dashing, prestigious and suitable publisher, Prestige Books, for the publication of this book.

Dr. Ram Manohar Lohia College **Shyam S. Agarwalla**
Ranchi

A Suitable Boy: Vikram Seth's Magnum Opus

F.R. Leavis gives one of his most important explanations of how Dickens—or any novelist—provides a creative definition of 'life,' and concurrently gives a lucid statement of his own use of the word 'life': "'Life,' it may be commented, is a large word. Certainly it is a word we can't do without and unquestionably an important one, and the importance is of a nature that makes it obviously futile to try to define abstractly, by way of achieving precision, the force of value it has as I have just used it. We feel the futility the more intensely in that, as we consider Dickens's art in *Little Dorrit*, we see very patently at work a process that it seems proper to call definition by creative means."[1]

It is this kind of creative defining of life in the concrete that gives literature its importance, and Leavis emphasizes that the process of definition the artist provides is a very form of thought (if not the only real form) anti-theoretical. He insists that Dickens's capacity for effective thought about life is indistinguishable from his genius as a novelist. He further says: "Dickens's essential 'social criticism,' his inquest into Victorian civilization is inseparable from this process."[2]

Vikram Seth's *A Suitable Boy*[3] is an effective thought about life—the life not in slices but the life in its totality, in the Nehruvian era of Indian civilization. The writers of Indian English literature of the pre-Nehru era were nationalist in themes and outlook and very often used the myths of "superior" Indian mysticism and spiritualism to create our national identity during the Freedom Movement. But the writers of the nineties are likely to shrug off these in favour of the India of today and tomorrow in all its multifaceted profile. Amitav Ghosh, Upamanyu Chatterjee, Shashi Tharoor, Nina Sibal, Partap Sharma, Nayantara Sahgal and Vikram Seth concern themselves with contemporary reality and are unselfconsciously Indian in their use of English.

Each of them, with the exception of Seth, attempts to portray a slice of life. Ghosh, in his *Circle of Reason*, deals with the impact of science on the Indian mind. His second novel, *The Shadow Lines*, continues the concerns of the first novel. The boy narrator's growth to maturity takes place through a journey into a web of memories, not just his own but his cousin Tridib's, in which the personal events overlap with the historical events: the London of 1939, Dhaka torn by a civil war in the post-partition period, and a riot in Calcutta.

Chatterjee's *English, August* though subtitled *An Indian Story*, was not very Indian. To experience the kind of isolation and alienation that the hero, Agastya, feels, one needs to be educated in a Christian missionary school and to be part of the English-speaking (and therefore affluent) minority that is to be found in India's metropolitan centres. His second book, *The Last Burden*, moves on to more elemental emotions and experiences, a preoccupation with the mystery of death and the complexities of inter-personal relationships within the family. But Jamun, the hero of the novel, does not mark much of a change from Agastya.

Shashi Tharoor, in his *The Great Indian Novel*, writes "about Indian myths, legends, traditions, and present politics."[4] For him Draupadi is a metaphor for Indian democracy and the attempt to disrobe her in the *Mahabharata* is a reflection of what was attempted to be done to Indian democracy. About his narrator, Ved Vyas, Tharoor says: "my narrator had to be a sort of retired, venerable politician who has been through the nationalist movement, who has seen it all, done it all, and has strong opinions about everything. . . . In a sense I enjoyed the literary device of making him both a teller of the story and a participant in the action at critical moments"[5]

Nina Sibal's first novel, *Yatra*, is about Krishna's search for identity which is counterpoised against the background of her uncle's terrorist activities aimed against the British in the 1920s, the war in East Pakistan in 1971, and India's involvement in it, the Chipko movement, and the intrigues of the evil politician Chimanlal Bajaj.

Partap Sharma's first novel, *Days of the Turban* (1988), "set against the background of fact," deals with the rise of terrorism in the Punjab in the larger historical context, ranging from the Muslim invasion from the north to British rule and culminating in the Partition of the state of Punjab, and indeed of the country.

Compared to Ghosh, Chatterjee, Tharoor, Sibal and Sharma, Seth's first novel in prose, *A Suitable Boy*, is all-encompassing, a 'magnum opus' of social comedy in the great tradition of Jane Austen, Charles Dickens and R.K. Narayan, interlaced with the political realism of Graham Greene and Nayantara Sahgal. Sandwiched between the social comedy and the political realism is the murky and intriguing academic world of Professor Mishra and Professor Pran, in the line of Srilal Shukla's *Raag Darbari*.

Of the art of Jane Austen, Legouis and Cazamian write: "The secret complexities of self-love, the many vanities, the imperceptible quiverings of selfishness, all that a Rochefoucauld had shown us in the strong and bitter note of straightforward denunciation . . . is here indicated or suggested so calmly and with so sober a touch that the author's personal reaction is reduced to a minimum."[6] The crass materialism starting from the time of Elizabeth, at the time of Industrial Revolution resulted in the polarization of village society between the haves and have-nots. "By the end of the eighteenth century, after industrialization had made its appearance, these things were to culminate in a manner which has been called tragic, and the tragedy can be seen as a theme in the poetry of George Crabbe, the poetry and prose of John Clare, the paintings of Gorge Morland and the descriptions of the labouring poor made by the clergyman David Davies."[7] And Crabbe was the contemporary and favourite of Austen. Little wonder, Austen produced Mrs. Bennett and Mr. Collins, on the one hand, and Darcy and Lady Catherine de Bourgh, on the other.

Just as the Industrial Revolution affected the England of Austen, Nehru's socialist and industrial revolution affected the India of the fifties. Nirad C. Chaudhari, a sharp observer of Indian scene writes: "A far stronger force, in actual fact the only positive force, is the Hindu's insatiable greed for money. . . . It is this love of money which is the true motive behind the industrialization of India."[8]

An outcome of the industrialization in England and India, the insatiable greed for money, led to the birth of a lower middle class. Mrs. Bennett and Mrs. Rupa Mehra, members of this class, find it increasingly difficult to search suitable boys for their daughters. In to-day's India, this social problem has assumed a monstrous form, where thousands of dear daughters are burnt for inadequate dowry. No contemporary Indian writing in English has cared to probe the miseries and agonies of mothers of many daughters, with scant resources and who are bogged down in the quagmire of caste, religion and tradition. Vikram Seth, basically an English brown Sahib, sitting away from the growing and unfulfilling aspirations and consequent frustrations of this middle class, writes marvellously on this theme. This alone places him in the great tradition of Austen, Dickens and Narayan.

As mentioned above, one of the themes of this great novel is Mrs. Mehra, in search of a suitable boy for her dear daughter, Lata, and Lata's unconcern for the concern of her obsessional and hysterical mother. The medium is comedy. Comedy, in the words of Meredith, is deeply concerned with appearance, with the deepening up of appearances, and also with the shattering of shams. The connection between this kind of humour and the humour of the Jonsonian comedy is well-known commonplace of literary criticism. A tentative definition of the humour through characterization in Austen, Dickens and Seth is that it is something we get whenever a character makes us laugh by himself or herself. He or she has been clearly placed before us once for all, and need not do anything in particular, except go on. Take Mrs. Bennett of Austen's *Pride and Prejudice.* Her sole concern in life is to marry her five daughters off to five suitable boys (in her eyes) and for that she, days in and days out, roams about in her small village, monitors the comings and goings of all eligible bachelors, prods Mr. Bennett to think of them. In *A Suitable Boy* Mr. Mehra is dead and, therefore, is immune to Mrs. Mehra's reports, searches and pleadings. But she invokes "Him" whenever the situation arises because for her, "late Raghubir Mehra still inhabited the form in which she had known him when he was alive." (3) Take, for instance, her fond remembrance of Mr. Mehra on the wedding day of her daughter Savita: "'If He had been here, I would have worn the tissue patola sari I wore for my own wedding,' sighed Mrs. Rupa Mehra." (3) Capital letters, "He," "His," and "Him," usually used for God, are used lavishly for late Raghubir Mehra and this produces peals of laughter; for it shows her stupidity, hypocrisy and boorishness.

The search of Mrs. Bennett for five eligible bachelors for her five daughters and the search of Mrs. Mehra for a suitable boy for her suitable daughter are like pilgrim's progress. Like pilgrims, they piously, religiously and dutifully devote their entire time to reach only one goal—the marriage of their daughters. This passionate search of Mrs. Mehra is unparalleled in the history of Indian writers writing in English and thus Austen and Seth are a class by themselves.

Unlike Thomas Hardy and E.M. Forster, Austen and Seth examine the society of their times by tools of humour. And they create humour through characters. We quote some passages from Austen and Seth to substantiate our point:

> "My dear Mr. Bennett!" replied his wife, "how can you be so tiresome! You must know that I am thinking of his marrying one of them."[9]
>
> "My dear, you flatter me. I certainly have had my share of beauty, but I do not pretend to be any thing extraordinary now. When a woman has five grown up daughters, she ought to give over thinking of her own beauty."[10]
>
> "Why are you trying to annoy me then I am so happy? And Pran and Savita will be happy, you will see. They will be happy," she said emphatically. (4)
>
> "I know what your hmms mean, young lady, and I can tell you I will not stand for hmms in this matter. I do know what is best. . . . Do you think it is easy for me, trying to arrange things for all four of my children without His help?" (3)

At this point, I cannot help myself quoting from Dickens's novel *Martin Chuzzlewit* to drive my contention to a conclusion: "Mrs. Gamp a lady of that happy temperament which can be ecstatic without any other stimulating cause than a general desire to establish a large and profitable concern." All these great comic characters—Mrs. Bennett, Mrs. Mehra and Mrs. Gamp—should be read, enjoyed and not examined as a pretender to any philosophy or message of life. They are the concretization of some abstractions like stupidity, hypocrisy and pomposity. It is, therefore, as frustrating to squeeze any message of life or philosophy from them as to expect Falstaff to do the same.

From Mrs. Bennett we go to Mrs. Gamp. Mrs. Gamp is drawn, in part at least, from life and has some bearing on real-life counterparts. She has Mrs. Harris who was "a phantom of Mrs. Gamp's brain . . . created for the express purpose of holding imaginary dialogues with her on all manner of subjects and invariably winding up with a compliment to the excellence of her nature."[11] E.M. Forster says that by the additional invention of Mrs. Harris the comic invention is all reproduced, acted over and with renewed spirit and doubled and quadrupled in her favour, and that this on the whole is the happiest stroke of humorous art in all the writings of Dickens. Mrs. Mehra's comic invention, 'His' and 'He' (for late Raghubir Mehra), and her invocation of 'Him' at the times of crisis and distress to silence her daughter, Lata, is a master stroke of Seth's fertile humour. Like Mrs. Harris, Mr. 'He' takes on fleeting flesh-and-blood form and that continues to be part of Mrs. Mehra's existence as a comic character in the novel.

Lata, the heroine of the novel, is a student of English literature at the University of Brahmpur, an invented city on the Ganges in the invented state of Purva Pradesh. She has three main suitors. Her first suitor, Kabir Durrani, is her fellow student, a cricketer and a Muslim. Though a "non-Khatri Hindu," (183) Lata falls in love with him, thinking him to be a suitable husband but Kabir's insistence on marrying her after two years clinches the issue.

> "Two years, I think. First I have to finish my degree. After that I'm going to apply to get into Cambridge or may be take the exam for the Indian Foreign Service—"
>
> "Ah—" It was a low cry of almost physical pain. He stopped, realizing how selfish he must have sounded.
>
> "I'll be married off in two years," said Lata, covering her face in her hands. "You're not a girl. You don't understand. My mother might not even let me come back to Brahmpur." (186)

Advances made by Amit Chatterjee towards Lata were abruptly stopped mid-way by her mother who had instantly taken a dislike for the Chatterjees. She says: "'I have no intention of accepting things as they come,' said Mrs. Rupa Mehra, the unsavoury vision of sacrificing yet another of her children on the altar of the Chatterjees making her flush with indignation." (482) Then, she shows her dislike for Amit: "She looked at Amit, and thought: Poet, Wastrel! He has never earned an honest rupee in his life. I will not have all my grandchildren speaking Bengali." (486)

In the case of Kabir and Amit, it is Lata who has found out suitable boys for herself but Kabir does not sense the difficulty of Lata—born and brought up in a conservative family, presided over by Mrs. Mehra and Amit is good-for-nothing, in the eyes of Mrs. Mehra for he is a poet and poets are dreamers. What is more, Mrs. Mehra finds his family ultra-modern, a minus point for a conservative like Mrs. Mehra. So, Mrs. Mehra finds out "a Khanna, he was bound to be a Khatri." (556) And the greatest advantage that he has over the other two, in the Nehruvian period of the fifties, is "a dowry (continued Kalpana in her curvaceously looped script), he isn't the kind of the man to ask for it, and there is no one to ask for it on his behalf." (562) Kalpana Gaur, the intermediary between them, writes to Haresh about the prospect of a matrimonial arrangement: "The point is that Mrs. Mehra has a young daughter Lata—and she was so impressed by you that she wanted to know if there was any possibility of anything being arranged between Lata and you by way of matrimony. . . . But she saw you that evening and was extremely impressed. She thinks it would be a boy of your type who would have made Lata's late father happy." (566) In this way the caravan of the matrimony of Lata and Haresh moves slowly but surely to a point when Haresh visits Mrs. Mehra and Lata. Mrs. Mehra immediately liked Haresh but Lata didn't. "Her first impression of him was that he was shorter than she had expected. The next—when he opened his mouth to speak—was that he had been chewing paan. . . . In fact paan did not go at all well with her idea of a husband." (569) Later on she frankly said to Haresh: "Haresh, I think we should meet and talk a little more before I make up my mind finally. It's the most important decision of my life. I need to be completely sure." (1146)

It was a convention in Elizabethan drama that characters may fall in love at first sight: a convention which stems from reality, and from the common and ancient thought habit that the sight is the chief and most powerful of the senses; that beauty, which represents in the general correspondence virtue, is a great attractive force; and that the will of man naturally abhors what is evil and is attracted to what is good. When, as commonly it is said of lovers. "At the first sight/They have changed eyes." (*Tempest*, I.ii.44) It is a natural process that is being described and enacted. Lata's love for Kabir and Amit is a natural process.

Let us share the inner thoughts of Lata for Kabir and Amit. About Amit she muses: "And what would it be like to be married to such a man? . . . He was just Amit—to convert him into a husband was absurd—the thought of it made Lata smile and shake her head." (1289) Kabir teases her by asking some inconvenient questions about her relationship with Amit:

> "And I suppose you go up and down the Hooghly on a boat at dawn."
>
> "Kabir—how dare you, you of all people. . . ." The color drained from Kabir's face. He grabbed her right hand and held it tight.
>
> "Let go" whispered Lata. "Let me go at once. Or I'll drop this plate." (1258)

Both Amit and Kabir are impractical lovers for Lata and she rejects their outer life of "telegrams and angers" (the phrase is taken from E.M. Forster's *Howards End*) in favour of the inner life of personal relations, actualities of material life, represented by Haresh. To help her in making up her mind, Haresh gives up his paan-chewing habit. He proudly asserts: "I am a practical man, and I am proud of it." (1290) D.H. Lawrence, in a letter to Forster, sharply reacts against Forster's 'glorification' of the Wilson: "You did make a nearly deadly mistake glorifying those business people in *Howards End*. Business is no good."[13] Seth, in the style of Forster, connects the prose of life with its poetry. Margaret, in Lata, triumphs over Helen. Seth beckons us 'to connect' the material with the romantic, the present with the past, the Hareshian qualities of action with Lataian sensitivity and love. Seth is certainly on the side of Lata but as a liberal humanist he is keen to show the redeeming features of Haresh also.

The family drama of the matrimonial quest is interwoven with the politics of the immediate post-independent India, 1951-52. Mahesh Kapur, Revenue Minister of Purva Pradesh, is a veteran freedom fighter, close to Pt. Nehru, and is radical and socialist, a sort of Ved Vyas of Shashi Tharoor. He is determined to abolish the feudal system of Zamindari in Purva Pradesh. His friend, the nawab, is stubbornly determined to fight him on this issue to protect what he has. Mr. S.S. Sharma, Chief Minister, an old freedom fighter, secular and aloof, is also a supporter of Pt. Nehru. L.N. Agarwal, traditionalist and obscurantist, is a follower of Purusottom Das Tandon. The Congress is divided into two camps—one led by Pt. Nehru at the national level and Sharma and Kapoor at the state level and the other led by Tandon, Agarwal and some others. P.C. Ghosh of Bengal, Kidwai and Pant of U.P. and Kripalani are often mentioned but they do not live in the novel.

Mahesh Kapur "works terribly late and sometimes comes back from the secretariat after midnight, dog tired. . . . Two hundred clauses, two hundred ulcers, she thinks." (217) He successfully pilots the Zamindari Abolition Bill in the state legislature and in the words of the Speaker: "The question before the House is that the Purva Pradesh Zamindari Abolition Bill of original date 1948 as passed by the Legislative Assembly, amended by the Legislative Council and further amended by the Legislative Assembly, be passed." (287) Politics for Mahesh Kapoor was a means to serve his people. In the words of Dr. Lohia: "Truth, work, generosity and other elements of character-building should become the primary concern of politics, not of course in their truncated form. . . . During all this political activity, man will have to learn to be generous and to base his whole being and action on the philosophy of good will. . . . Only then will politics acquire a part of that attraction which religion or art has always exercised for its quality of solace, of going beyond one's skin, of feeling whole and at peace."[14] But for politicians like Agarwal, "politics is like the coal trade. How can you blame people if their hands and faces become a little black?" (323) These coal traders, in the name of religion, serve their own interests and for them religion in politics is like hors-d'oeuvre. That is why corruption, in 1950-51, had begun to eat into the rationing system and the system of government contracts had surpassed anything known under the British. The police too had become more overt in their extortions. "Some local pujari locates a Shiva-linga in the Ganga," said Kedarnath. "It is supposed to have come from the Chandrachur Temple, the great Shiva temple that they say Aurangzeb destroyed. The pillars of the mosque do have bits of Hindu carving, so it must have been made out of some ruined temple, God knows how long ago." (198)

Politics, in Nayantara Sahgal's *This Time of Morning* (1965), is centred on the last years of Nehru's stewardship of India. The rot, decay, bigotry and corruption, set in the prime years of the Nehru period in *A Suitable Boy*, reaches its zenith in *This Time of Morning*. Much of the action in Nayantara Sahgal's novel takes place in Delhi and much of the action in Vikram Seth's novel takes place in Brahmpur, the former real and the latter fictitious. Personal and political ambitions criss-cross, and there are unpredictable affiliations and separations in both the novels.

This leads us to examine the exchanges between Doctor Eduardo Plarr and his friend and patient, the once-popular South American novelist Jorge Julio Saavedra in Greene's *The Honorary Consul*. These exchanges take the form for the most part of a socio-comic debate about realism and abstraction in fiction. The debate, introduced fairly early on in the book, turns with characteristically quizzical irony on the problem of making a novel both politically topical and timeless. "If one is to write a political novel of lasting value," Saavedra says, "it must be free from all the petty details that date it. Assassinations, kindnapping, the torture of prisoners—these things belong to our decade. But I do not want to write merely for the seventies."[15] Saavedra expands: "A poet— the true novelist must always be in his way a poet—a poet deals in absolutes. . . . A novelist today who wants to represent tyranny should not describe the activities of General Stroessner in Paraguay—that is journalism not literature. Tiberius is a better example of the poet."[16] As it turns out, Greene works his cunning to eat this particular cake and have it too by seeing to it, as often before, that those 'things of our decade' (assassination, kidnapping, the torture of political prisoners, revolutionary activism, all feature in some way in his story) shall exist in a symbiotic relationship with a particular kind of inquiry into the nature of certain absolutes. The terms of the inquiry are penetrated by that sense of the ambiguous surrounding concepts which human beings use often and understand little—their terms for them are love, honour, God—which gives to Greene's novels their unmistakable personal flavour. "My own novels," says Nayantara Sahgal, "are about how the idealism of an emergent nation has withered and rotted in corruption and decay."[17]

Vikram Seth like Greene and Sahgal writes about a decade, the fifties, and more precisely about the period, 1950-51. He shows the India of withering idealism, rotting corruption, pestering communal disharmony, parasitical intrigue of politicians, the perpetual fight between the forces of progress and modernity and the forces of tradition and obscurism. Take, for instance, the conversation of Maan with Netaji:

> After a pause, Netaji said, "You must have a lot of contacts."
> "Contacts?"
> "Yes, contacts, contacts, you know what I mean."
> "But—"
> "You should use your contacts to help us," said Netaji bluntly. "I'm sure you could get me a kerosene dealer's licence. That should be easy enough for the Revenue Minister's son."
> "Actually, all that is under a different ministry," said Maan, unoffended. "Civil Supplies, I think." "Come on, that doesn't matter. I know how it works." (617)

This conversation is only one of the many examples of the withering idealism of the pre-independent India and the rotting corruption of the immediate post-independent India, when the modern netas try every means to notch up licences in the commodity-starved country to live lives of luxuries and comforts, at the expense of millions of people living below poverty-line. This tendency to curry favours with ministers, their progenies, their minions;

has increased over the years in India and to-day no work is done without a nod from a minister or his minion.

If Mahesh Kapoor is progressive and secular, his cabinet colleague, L.N. Agarwal, is obscurantist and communalist. Agarwal strongly supported the reconstruction of the Shiva Temple and the Muslims resisted it with all vehemence. "In sharp contrast to L.N. Agarwal, Mahesh Kapoor, though a Hindu, was well-known for his tolerance towards other religions . . . and was liked and respected among knowledgeable Muslims." (620) But the elevation of Agarwal to the post of Chief Minister of Purva Pradesh, finally seals the fate of the forces of progress and liberalism.

As the novel progresses, no stone of social India is left unturned and, therefore, naturally it also discusses another hot topic of the early fifties, the condition of the Scheduled Castes. "Well, my sister says that the jatavs tried to force themselves onto the local Ramlila Committee this year. They said that at least one of the five swaroops should be selected from scheduled caste boys. Naturally, no one listened to them at all. But it could spell trouble." (1035) The call of Gandhi to abolish untouchability and the relentless war of Ambedkar against Chaturvarna find their echoes in these lines.

Politics have changed dramatically from good to bad, from service to people to service to self, in the immediate first four or five years of independence and have a stage in which "Those people who broke their heads fighting for freedom are now breaking each other's. And we have new entrants to the business. If I were a criminal, for example, and I could get into politics profitably and without much difficulty, I would not say: 'I can deal in murder or drugs, but politics is sacred.' It would be no more sacred to me than prostitution." (1284) Nayantara Sahgal's *Rich Like Us*, "which grew out of her involvement with the movement for civil liberties during the Emergency, is a story of a generation who remember the British Raj and Partition, and cherish the ties of family, caste and religion because they offer a continuity with the past. But it is also the story of the India of the 1970s which is guided by what has become an ideology of corruption. The conjunction of the two stories produces an admirable construct of ambivalence towards history in which idealism and corruption jostle with each other."[18] *A Suitable Boy* is also about a generation which remembers the British Raj and the Partition and cherishes the ties of family, caste and religion because they offer a continuity with the past. It is also a story of the India of the early fifties which is guided by communal disharmony, caste discord, hierarchical social order and love for worldly pleasures. It is also the story of idealism of Nehru and Kapoor jostling with the ideology of corruption. Then, there are long parliamentary exchanges and commentaries which are parts of history books. One can emphatically say that the novels of Sahgal and Seth, meandering through many political events of the India of the seventies and the early fifties respectively, could not rise to the dizzy heights of *The Honorary Consul*. There is a God in their novels but He does not arbitrate among feuding groups. Love and honour are there but are adulterated by caste, religion and self-interest. Much as they try to extricate themselves from the bog of journalism, and they succeed partially, they are dated.

Into the social comedy and political realism of the novel is added the academic skullduggery. Of this academic skullduggery, Paul Johnson says, "It is a myth that universities are nurseries of reason. They are hot houses for every kind of extremism, irrationality, intolerance and prejudice, where intellectual and social snobbery is almost purposefully instilled." Pran Kapoor, an asthmatic university lecturer in English, is determined to get James Joyce on the university syllabus; Professor Mishra is resolved on keeping the Irishman out. "Professor Mishra was a huge, pale, oily husk, political and manipulative to the very depths of his being." (49) He loved power and authority like L.N. Agarwal and Mahesh Kapoor. The principal of *Raag Darbari* is the prototype of Prof. Mishra or vice-versa. Pran is the prototype of Master Khanna. Pran and Prof. Mishra represent modernity and tradition, sincerity and authority and pro-changers and anti-changers. Prof. Mishra tries to elbow Pran out by self-congratulation, by his veiled hint to ease him out of the syllabus committee and the race for readership of the university department but Pran retorts, "I wouldn't do it." (794) With a mixture of guile and sweet, characteristics of a good politician—Prof. Mishra says— "Your health, my dear boy. I am only thinking of your own health.

You are driving yourself too hard. All these articles you've been publishing." (794)

The intellectual snobbery of Prof. Mishra and the humility of Pran are also evident in the bridge party hosted by Dr. Kishen Chand Seth. Professor Mishra defines "three kind of teachers: those who are forgotten, those who are remembered and hated, and the third, the lucky ones, and I hope I am one of them, those who are remembered and—he paused—forgiven." (831) A perfect pecksniff.

Our academics cease to read and write once they become senior professors or head a department. The mad rush to be on this committee or that, to boss over or to show off, and, to increase "factionalism through arguments and abuse, kicks and shoe-beatings, literature and the arts, and all other means,"[19] have disfigured our temples of learning. Let me quote the conversation between Prof. Mishra and Dr. Ila Chattopadhyay.

> "Many months ago, my dear lady,"—he turned towards her—"I remember how impressed I was by reading your work on the Metaphysicals. That was long before I sat on the committee which—"
>
> "Well, we're neither of us young now," interrupted Dr. Ila Chattopadhyay, "and neither of us has published anything of worth in the last ten years. I wonder why that is."
>
> While Professor Mishra was still recovering from this remark, Professor Jaikumar put forth an explanation which caused him a different kind of pain. "Our typical young university teacher," he began, "is overworked when he is junior—he has to teach elementary prose and compulsory Yinglish. If he is yinnately conscientious, he has no time for yennything else. By then the fire is out—"
>
> "If it was ever there," added Dr. Ila Chattopadhyay. (1272)

That our university teachers, in the words of Paul Johnson, resort to irrationality, is evident from the remarks of Professor Jaikumar: "Ripeness is not all. Perhaps, ripe in years, and thinking he academically now knows yevrything, our university teacher turns from knowledge to religion that goes beyond knowledge—from gyaan to bhakti. Rationality has a very tenuous hold on the Indian psyche." (1273)

The selection of Pran for the readership of the university is stoutly blocked by Professor Mishra, in the meeting of the selection committee, on one pretext or another, but one thing is clear that he does it out of prejudice. It is only the stubborn determination of the external expert, Dr. Chattopadhyay and the wrong calculation of Mahesh Kapoor's probable victory in the election to Legislative Assembly by Badri—that compels Prof. Mishra to agree to the selection of Pran. But hypocrisy does not desert Prof. Mishra even at the time of his defeat and he deftly turns his defeat into victory. He tells Pran: "It was a close thing, a very close thing. Some of the other candidates were truly excellent, but, well, I believe we have an understanding, you and I, an equation, as it were. . . . There was opposition. Some people said you were too young, too untried. . . . But quite apart from the question of merit, at such a sad time for your family one feels a sense of obligation, one feels one has to do one's bit. I am not one who talks of humanity in exaggerated terms, but, well—was it not the great Wordsworth who talked about those 'little nameless unremembered acts of kindness and of love.'" (1277-78) See, for example, Pecksniff's pious resolve at the Chuzzlewit family gathering ("Charity, my dear, . . . when I take my chamber candlestick to-night, remind me to be more than usually particular in praying for Mr. Anthony Chuzzlewit; who has done me an injustice"). Or, read the speech of Vaidyaji: "To say, now, right here and this very moment, you will have to resign! I am not saying this in anger but careful consideration. I am saying it for your benefit, for the benefit of the college and for the benefit of the whole of society."[20] Vikram Seth satirizes brilliantly the academic world of the early fifties and Srilal Shukla of the late fifties.

The comic world of Mrs. Mehra, the political world of Kapoor, Agarwal and netaji, the academic world of Prof. Mishra and Pran and the poetical and prosaic worlds of Lata are the major sources of the creative defining of life by Vikram Seth. A novel, containing upwards of 6,00,000 words, hundreds of characters from various walks of life, their habits, speeches, minds and characteristics, and, what is more, the faithful description of the India of 1951-52, can be compared with some of the classics of the world literature, say *War and Peace, Dr. Zhivago* and *Martin Chuzzlewit*. In this novel, comedy plays sprightly with satire, poetry with prose (Forsterian style), politics with religion, politics with academe, melodrama with realism and boxwallas with shoe makers. Truly, *A Suitable Boy* is the magnum opus of this decade.

NOTES

1. F.R. Leavis and Q.D. Leavis, *Dickens the Novelist* (Harmondsworth: Penguin, 1972), p. 285.
2. *Ibid.*, p. 297.
3. *A Suitable Boy* (New Delhi: Viking), p. 4.
4. Shashi Tharoor, "Writer at Work," *Gentleman*, 1990, p. 46.
5. *Ibid.*, p. 51.
6. *The History of English Literature*, p. 965.
7. Peter Laslett, *The World We have Lost* (Methuen, 1985), p. 195.
8. *The Continent of Circe* (Bombay: Jaico), pp. 83-84.
9. Jane Austen, *Pride and Prejudice*, p. 2.
10. *Ibid.*, p. 5.
11. Charles Dickens, *Martin Chuzzlewit* (Oxford: O.U.P.), p. 348.
12. R.A. Foakes, "The Player's Passion," *Essays and Studies* (1954), p. 66.
13. *The Letters of D.H. Lawrence*, ed. Aldous Huxley (22-9-1222), p. 552.
14. *Interval during Politics*, K.S. Karanth (Bombay: Sindhu), p. 35.
15. Graham Greene, *The Honorary Consul* (New York: Pocket Books), p. 58.
16. *Ibid.*, p. 59.
17. "Some Thoughts on the Puzzle of Identity," *The Journal of Commonwealth Literature*, Vol. XXIX, No. 1, 1993, p. 10.
18. Devindra Kohli, "A Tragic Love Affair? The Contemporary Indian-English Scene," *Aspects of Commonwealth Literature*, Vol. 1, Oct. 1988-June 1989, p. 10.
19. Srilal Shukla, *Raag Darbari*, English trans. Gillian Wright (New Delhi: Penguin), p. 75.
20. *Ibid.*, p. 337.

Critical Response to *A Suitable Boy*: A Scrutiny

A Suitably Boy, even before its publication, generated a great deal of interest and high expectations. Its publication two years ago led to a wide variety of response. David Myers, in his perceptive essay on *A Suitable Boy*, claims that the novel would be a comparative failure without some scenes of tragic suffering; he, particularly, pinpoints the harrowing evocation of Mrs. Kapoor's cremation and the sense of loss and tragic guilt that Mahesh Kapoor and his son, Maan Kapoor, suffer from.[1] I have no reason to doubt Myers's love for Indian culture but I wonder whether he has ventured to go deep into various aspects of Indian culture.

In Hinduism, death does not provoke tragic scenes, like it does in Islam and Christianity. Hindus accept death as the certain end of the dead man's or woman's personality. The lament at a Hindu funeral says, "That which has spoken has gone—the spirit has departed." The incapacity or desperate refusal to acquiesce in the finality of death and the notion of the survival, reappearance, and transmission of the soul or spirit runs like a spinal cord through the whole connected series of the beliefs that are comprised in Hinduism. The description of the cremation of Mrs. Mehra (17-27) is not harrowing as Myers would like us to believe. *Le denil est un culte* ("Mourning is worship"). The ceremonies, the honours, attentions, mournings and prayers, in *A Suitable Boy* for the dead Mrs. Mehra, are not for the dead woman but addressed to her, that the funeral service was usually an offer or an attempt to do her service. The collection of ash and bones and carrying them back first to the dead person's house, and then to a holy river, like the Ganga at Brahmpur, is another deep-rooted belief among Hindus that as bodily death is giving up of the ghost, he or she must be provided with a fresh tenement, or at least with some temporary accommodation.

Alfred C. Lyall, citing an example of one Hurdeo Lala, poisoned in Central India by his brother through jealousy, clears the mist of misreading of Indian culture and says, "This was a sensational murder, not unlike that of Hamlet's father; and whereas in England he might have been commemorated by a tragic drama, a mournful ballad, or by a figure in a wax-work exhibition, in India temples were erected to him."[2]

In another paragraph, Myers writes, "The husband [Mahesh Kapoor] has to perceive that his wife's life, which she devoted modestly to her 'puja,' to her magnificent garden and to her family and friends, has been spiritually superior to his life which he has committed to politics, ambition, secularity and mocking contempt for his wife's piety."[3] Myers calls it a tragic scene. But if he cares to delve deep into Indian history, he will find example of unobtrusive and often hidden by the purdah, from the earliest days, women of strong character, of robust practical sagacity, the inspirers often, the succourers always, of men. Ahilyabai and Pandita Rambai—to name only two—who never have been lacking such broad-minded, steadfast, capable, managers, whether it be of a kingdom or of a household, who spread round about them order and contentment and trust. Mrs. Kapoor is steeped in the tradition of Ahilyabai and Pandita Rambai.

The difference of approach to this world, by Mr. Kapoor and Mrs. Kapoor, is as transparent as the difference of approach of Pt. Jawahar Lal Nehru, the political mentor of Mahesh Kapoor and Kamala Nehru. "Indeed, for all the Minister of Revenue's impatience with her, she was his regret. And it was right that she should continue to be so, for he should have treated her better while she lived, the poor, ignorant, grieving fool."[4] Nehru says of Kamala, "We were attracted to each other . . . but our backgrounds were different and there was a want of adjustment. These maladjustments would sometimes lead to friction."[5] Contrary to the argument of Myers, there is not much of transformation in Mahesh Kapoor, after the death of his wife. His soliloquy reveals his mind, "He wanted to give up and let the world take care of itself. But he could not let Maan go; and politics had been his life."

(1225) Nehru writes of his wife's death, "I was with my wife when she died in Lausanne on February 28, 1936. A little while before news had reached me that I had been elected President of the Indian National Congress for the second time. I returned to India."[6] There are traces of sadness in Mahesh Kapoor and Pt. Nehru, but not of remorse and guilt.

A tragedy, in the Greek drama, is how to grapple with the problem of evil. Why does man suffer? Why is there evil in the world? The enigma of religion, of God. What a pitiful thing is man, child of a day, with his blind and aimless strivings against all-powerful fate. There is nothing comparable to the power and majesty of Greek tragedy in Sanskrit. In Hinduism, nobody challenges commonly-held patterns of religious faith. Among these were the doctrines of rebirth and cause and effect. Accident or evil without cause were ruled out, for what happens now is the necessary result of some previous happening in a former life. Writing of Shudraka's *Mrichhkatika,* staged in New York in 1924, Joseph Wood Krutch says, "Macbeth and Othello, however great and stirring they might be, are barbarous heroes because the passionate tumult of Shakespeare is the tumult produced by the conflict between a newly acquired sensibility and a series of ethical concepts inherited from the savage age." Indians have long ago settled this tumult and, therefore, have created a civilization which has reached stability. Mahesh Kapoor, Maan Kapoor and Pt. Nehru are the products of this stable civilization and, therefore, the question of tragedy, on the death of near and dear ones, does not arise.

Reviewing *A Suitable Boy,* Firdaus Kanga says, "Too many characters share the same sensibility, gentle and fuzzy and slightly overemotional, so that the old Nawab sounds much like the old minister, one widow much like another and all good wives are just as good."[7] After all is said about English flourishing in India, it still remains a 'foreign' tongue as far as the lower classes and vast rural population are concerned. Despite the mushroom growth of English-medium schools in India and the propensity of urban middle classes to admit their sons and daughters into them, the fact remains that English, for most educated Indians, is a means to earn a fine living. Amaresh Datta writes of creative writers, writing in English in India, and says, "But one may still wonder if English can become the language of our dreams, of the nuances of our social and personal relationships and of elemental passions oriented in a particular way by our environment and tradition. In any case, the literature produced by Indian authors in English cannot perhaps avoid some kind of artificiality whether it centres round non-Indian experience or Indian."[8] It may be true that "many of the key words and images in which the Indian sensibility lies embedded may be found to be just untranslatable."[9] Both the statements are half true. A perceptive critic, teacher, and novelist Prema Nandakumar, replying to the criticism that her characters, in *Atom and the Serpent* spoke in the same style, says, "But then, almost everyone in a university speaks alike. They all handle English with the same straight sentences and predictable pomposities. However, it is quite a different experience when they switch over to their mother tongues."[10] Along with translating key words and images associated with Indian sensibility, Vikram Seth also conveys the sensibility, symbolizing these words and thus creates an epic.

Another reviewer, James Buchan, says, "Why Lata—a sweet creation, if sometime forced, by the literary burden she's carrying, into speechlessness—chooses the suitor she chooses is not clear."[11] In the aftermath of the horrible Indian partition and the resultant communal frenzy, in 1951-52, it was unthinkable, on the part of Vikram Seth, to show an inter-religious marriage between Kabir Durrani and Lata. Even in 1995, the showing of the marriage of a Muslim girl with a Hindu boy in *Bombay,* directed by Mani Ratnam, has raised dust of controversy, among Hindus and Muslims. Advancing reasons for Lata's not marrying Kabir, Caryl Campbell says: "Lata, a Hindu, knows that she cannot marry a Muslim, and she also realizes, or he persuades herself, perhaps with more prescience that is entirely convincing that romantic love is not necessarily the best prelude to marriage."[12] David Myers suggests another reason for the rejection of Kabir by Lata: it is her rejection of passion from her life. She rejects Amit Chatterjee. She muses, "And what would it be like to be married to such a man? . . . He was just Amit—to convert him into a husband was absurd—the thought of it made Lata smile and shake her head." (1289) He, steeped deep in his Muse, would be unable to shoulder the materialistic and marital responsibilities and would prove to be more a burden than an asset. So, the only person left is Haresh. She chooses Haresh because he was not only a hardworking, uncouth, intelligent and pusher but also a symbol of "a new India—an ambitious, pragmatic, anti-snobbish, working-class, self-made Indian man."[13] He was Mr. Wilcox to Margaret.

According to Malcolm Bradbury, *A Suitable Boy* "is a vast chronicle novel of post-Independence Indian life, and one of the more startling works of the early nineties."[14]

Vikram Seth talks to Amit Roy about the genesis of *A Suitable Boy*: "I wanted to write about India. I planned to write a series of five short novels. Instead, I wrote one rather long novel which deals with a period I did not, at first, think was very interesting—the early 1950s." He thought that after dealing swiftly with this period, he would "go forward to the Sino-Indian war, the Emergency and all that kind of stuff. Instead, I got stuck in that period."[15]

The more he researched the period, the more the topics obsessed him—"Zamindari abolition, courtesans losing their sources of income, the British having left and the new kind of politicians coming in. The old politicians who had been self-sacrificing now becoming more self-serving."

Is there a Lata in his own life? Seth gets agitated at this line of questioning. "No, I can't talk about that kind of stuff," he replies, a trifle huffily. He is not married.

Two important points emerge from this talk. First, Seth wanted to write another *Midnight's Children*, clothed in social realism. Second, we venture into the realm of possibility and say that Seth must have either encountered a Lata or he has made a mental picture of a girl, like Lata, whom he would ultimately marry.

NOTES

1. David Myers, "Vikram Seth's Epic Renunciation of the Passions: Deconstructing Moral Codes in *A Suitable Boy*" in *Indian Literature Today*, R.K. Dhawan, ed. (New Delhi: Prestige, 1994), Vol. I.

2. Alfred Lyall, "Natural Religion in India," in "Rede Lectures" at Cambridge (1891), "Asiatic Studies: Second Series."
3. David Myers, p. 100.
4. Vikram Seth, *A Suitable Boy* (London: Viking, 1993), p. 1220.
5. Jawaharlal Nehru, *An Autobiography* (New Delhi: O.U.P., 1989), p. 561.
6. *Ibid.*, p. 600.
7. Firdaus Kanga, "The Leaden Echo," *Poetry Review*, Spring 1993, Vol. 83, No. 1, p. 68.
8. Amaresh Datta, "The Other Person," *Indian Literature*, No. 144, July-August 1991, p. 100.
9. *Ibid.*, p. 97.
10. Prema Nandakumar, "Choosing a Linguistic Medium," *Indian Literature*, No. 145, Sept.-Oct. 1991, p. 16.
11. James Buchan, "A Foreign Country is the Past," *The Spectator*, 27 March 1993, p. 31.
12. Caryl Campbell, "*A Suitable Boy* (Review)," *In-between: Essays and Studies in Literary Criticism*, IV (March 1995), pp. 77-80.
13. David Myers, p. 84.
14. Malcolm Bradbury, *The Modern British Fiction* (London: Secker and Warbury, 1993; rep. 1994), p. 427.
15. Interview with Amit Roy, *The Telegraph* (Calcutta), 29 August 1992.

Something is Rotten...:
A Political Analysis of *A Suitable Boy*

The play *Hamlet* is about a corrupt king in a corrupt polity—"Something is rotten in the state of Denmark." The novel *A Suitable Boy* is about a reasonably honest Prime Minister running a corrupt polity, in India, in the late forties and early fifties.

How do we define corruption? We may, for example, speak of physical corruption, moral corruption, corruption in the arts, and political corruption. Is there any general principle to bring these various kinds of corruption within one framework? Is there a link between moral and political corruption? For instance, Mark Antony is corrupted by power and then by his blind passion for Cleopatra. *Hamlet,* besides a corrupt polity, is also about the moral corruption of a King and a Queen:

> Nay, but to live
> In the rank sweat of an enseamed bed
> Stewed in corruption, honeying, and making love
> Over the nasty sky.   III, iv, 92-5

This was the charge made against the Court of James I: that it was corrupt both politically and morally.

The Gandhian age witnessed the tidal wave of untapped patriotism flowing in the barren land, irrigating the whole of it, and, producing the bumper crops of patriots, freedom-fighters, honest and zealous leaders, turbulent and serene followers, ready to sacrifice everything that they had—body, property, money and time. Literature is the mirror of the age. Gandhi's leadership was based on values, ethics, morals, spirituality, truth and non-violence. Therefore, the Gandhian age produced leaders like Sardar Patel, Nehru, Maulana Azad, Dr. Prasad, Acharya Kripalani, Purusuttomdas Tandon, C. Rajagopalachari, Subhash Chander Bose and innumerable other leaders, unprecedented in the recorded history of India. Naturally, this age also produced some of the finest writings in English, Hindi, Bengali, Tamil, Telugu, Gujarati and other regional languages. In English, writers like K.S. Venkataramani, R.K. Narayan, Mulk Raj Anand, Bhabani Bhattacharya and Raja Rao; in Hindi, Prem Chand, Nirala, Mahadevi Verma and Harivansh Rai Bachchan; Sarat Chandra, Bharati, Vallathol, Keshavasut, Mardhekar, Iqbal and Jigar, to mention a few towering peaks in the regional languages, reached the pinnacles of literature. Among politicians, Sarojini Naidu, C. Rajagopalachari and Jawaharlal Nehru were titans, in the Indian literary scene. Gandhi himself was a wordsmith, an artist in language, in Gujarati and English. Of him, Anwar, in Khwaja Ahmad Abbas's novel *Inqilab* (1955) says: "Now he knew why they called him Mahatma—a Great Soul. On his face was a look of suffering, kindness and pity, as if he personally felt the misery of every single human being. But there was also infinite calm and serenity and the boy's spirits revived as he looked into those gentle eyes." In the words of S. Radhakrishnan, a philosopher-statesman, was "This little man [Gandhi], so frail in appearance, was a giant among men, measured by the greatness of his soul. By his side other men, very important and famous men, big in their own way, big in their space and time, look small and insignificant. His profound sincerity of spirit, his freedom from hatred and malice, his mastery over himself, his human, friendly, all-embracing charity, his strong conviction which he shared with the great ones of history that the martyrdom of the body is nothing compared with the defilement of the soul, a conviction which he successfully put to the test in many dramatic situations, show the impact of religion on life, the impact of the eternal values on the sifting problems of the world of time."

Politics, in one sense, is concerned with the sifting problems of the world of time or, rather a part of it. Gandhi's politics had the stamp of spirituality which had nothing to do with either personal power or physical comfort. This led Middleton Murry to write on him: "Persons in power should be very careful how they deal with a man who cares nothing for sensual pleasure, nothing for riches, nothing for comfort or praise or promotion, but is simply determined to do what he believes to be right." Gandhi was Congress and the Congress fought for political freedom, social upliftment, moral regeneration and economic freedom and thus, gained political freedom on 15 August 1947.

The political freedom, all of a sudden, converted agitators into rulers, bureaucrats into public servants, the lathi-wielding police into friends and ruled into rulers. The Inqilab and the Bande Mataram reluctantly yielded place to Jan Gan Man. The Nehru Age had arrived. Gandhi died in 1948; Patel in 1950; and the socialists drifted away from the Congress, one by one. Nehru was the supreme boss of the party and of the Nation. *A Suitable Boy* is posited in the early years of our independence, 1951-52. The early years of the Nehruvian age started with a bang, like that of the Elizabethan age of the sixteenth century, full of bubbling optimism, robust vitality and great expectations. One of the chief factors was the presence of leaders of proven integrity, the other being the continuation of the services of "steel frame" bureaucracy. Nehru had wide choice in choosing able and trustworthy counsellors. Like Elizabeth I, he had a heart but it was always ruled by his head. He chose "men of stature, both in New Delhi and in the provincial capitals, who could not be lightly pushed aside. They were not the sort of men who would offer challenges to Jawaharlal Nehru's power; but within their own domains or bailiwicks, they would jolly well do what they liked."[2]

This is one side of the coin, the other being that of Nirad C. Chaudhuri. "In 1947, Nehru was fifty-eight in actual years, but in respect of ability to govern he was, like Louis XV, a child of five. Louis reigned for sixty-four years, it is forty-seven years since India got her independence. So, there are still left seventeen years for the parallelism I have drawn to be fully revealed."[3] In the last chapter of *The Autobiography of an Unknown Indian*, he wrote:

> The political history of India shows the Aryan, the Turk, the Turko-Mongol cum Persian as the only creators of political concepts and political orders in India up to the end of the seventeenth century, and after that the Anglo-Saxon take

their place. The rest have been only sterile imitators. In these intervals (imperial interregnums in which the natives of the country exercised political power) there have seen in India only a futile pursuit of the political concepts of the preceding foreign rulers, inefficient manipulation of the political machinery left by them, and, above all, an egregious aping of their arrogance and airs.[4]

Nehru aped the British and his followers and supporters aped him. Instead of following the Gandhian austerity and simplicity, Nehru aped his political predecessors. His moving into the Commander-in-Chief's residence, later called Teen Murti Bhawan, was a symbol of the new ruler's opulent mode of living. Chaudhuri labels politicians as Sons of Moloch and bureaucrats as Sons of Belial. The Sons of Moloch were no match for Sons of Belial. The latter, cunning egoists, exploited the core of egoism lurking in Sons of Moloch. "The crude Indian political leaders were no match for the sophisticated officials, who had also reached the lowest depth of sophistication, corruption."[5]

The word corruption means a condition of distortion and decay; while polis, and its adjective 'political' represent the state. If we consider the state to be a community of people joined together to preserve and enlarge the welfare of all its members, then we may define political corruption as the subversion of these interests for other ends, that is for one's private gain, or the gains of one's friends or of some other sectional group, or for some purpose contrary to the common welfare. Financial reward need not enter into these matters though it often does. What is more important is power. Those who govern the state have had power conferred upon them. Political corruption, in a word, is also the abuse of power.

Power is like heroin: the more the addicts take of it the more they need. If one goes by common experience he will find that heroin creates illusion and so does power. Power is never as great as it seems. The holder of the highest office in the state may see himself as the inspirer and Saviour of his people but to some he may seem no more than a devious, ambitious man whose lust for wealth and power debases the high office he holds. For instance,

Elizabeth's titles were The High and Mighty Prince, Elizabeth by the Grace of God Queen of England, Ireland and France, Defender of the Faith, Supreme Governor of the Church of England by law established, etc. But she seemed to some just a tetchy, vain old woman who had lived too long. Nehru is "Rituraj" for Tagore; "The Gentle Colossus" for Prof. Hiren Mukherjee; "he had the stature and beauty of a god," according to John Haynes Holmes. He was the spiritual heir of Gandhi, the Prime Minister of India, the world statesman, the Congress President, the voice of the newly-independent third world countries, the great writer and poet, the darling of the masses of India. On the other hand, in the late fifties, Devaprasad Ghosh, then President of the Bharatiya Jana Sangh (Rajya Sabha member, 1952-54) once said, "Neither Goa nor Kashmir is a problem of India. Pandit Nehru is the number one of India." In *A Suitable Boy*, Mahesh Kapoor, walking around his fields in Rudhia, ruminates about Nehru:

> Nehru sought to protect his policies as Prime Minister from any possible onslaught by the activist Congress President by proposing party resolutions on each of his main policies, all of which had been overwhelmingly passed by the assembled party. But passing resolutions by acclamation was one thing, controlling the personnel of the party—and the selection of candidates—another. Nehru was left with the uneasy sense that the lipservice that was being paid to the policies of his government would change once the right-wing got its own state of MLAs and MPs into parliament and the state legislatures. (954)

Nehru, therefore, did want to have a pliable and non-interfering President but Tandon as President "proved to be a formidable opponent in his own right. . . . And on every important issue his views were diametrically opposed to those of Nehru or his supporters—men such as Kripalani and Kidwai or, closer to Brahmpur, Mahesh Kapoor." (954) So, Nehru resigned from the "membership of the Congress Working Committee and the Central Election Board." (988) He "feels that the Congress is rapidly drifting away from its moorings." (989) Tandon was an organization man, seven years Nehru's senior and, like him, from Allahabad, a conservative, a man determined to impose "discipline and unity" (954) on recalcitrant party men. Nehru was a leader of the masses who "loved him and would almost certainly vote for him, as it had done ever since his great tour in the 1930s, when he had travelled around the country, charming and stirring up vast audiences." (955) Tandon was a brick-layer; Nehru was a pied piper. Both of them were the products of the National Movement, at the feet of Gandhi. Both were "vying with each other for power on the national stage." (953) The vacillating Nehru swiftly resigned from the Congress Working Committee and the Central Election Board. The Tandonites "smacked of the build-up to a showdown." (991) In a noble gesture and knowing fully well "the impropriety of Nehru's tactics," (992) Tandon resigned from the Congress Presidency. Nehru took over the Congress Presidency. "It was in effect a coup; and Nehru had won." (992)

The word 'coup' is defined as "a notable or successful stroke or move." (C.O.D.) The non-inclusion of Kidwai and Kripalani in the Congress Working Committee by Tandon was a strategy, an oblique way of attacking Nehru. Prior makes the point that "Bolingbroke's challenge to Mowbray is in effect an oblique way of attacking the king (Richard II),"[6] and he allows the advantages to Richard of Mowbray's banishment. The banishment of Kidwai and Kripalani from the Congress Working Committee by Tandon had given ample opportunity and advantage to Nehru to decry those who "wished to drive out from the Congress who did not fit in with their views or their general outlook." (989) Nehru surprised the Tandonites by his "most uncharacteristic unwillingness to back down, to understand their point of view, to postpone unpleasantness, to compromise." (991) Nehru according to his admirers, is a Hamlet but it does not correspond with this action of Nehru. He was not Hamlet, he was Richard II of Shakespeare. Regarding Richard II, Schoenbaum's comment is pertinent. He says: "I suggest that in Act I, in the council chamber at Windsor and at the lists in the Coventry, Richard displays as much political acumen as weakness, that his behaviour is not capricious but calculated, and that he does not fail but achieves a success necessarily limited by the realities of his situation."[7] "Shakespeare treats in a most sophisticated way the manipulation of power in a poker game where the stakes are exceedingly high."[8] Seth treats in a most sophisticated way the manipulation of power in a poker game between the Tandonites and the Nehruites where the stakes are exceedingly high.

The essence of this game percolates through the Centre to a State, i.e. Purva Pradesh. In Purva Pradesh, Mr. L.N. Agarwal, Home Minister, is a Tandonite whereas Mr. Mahesh Kapoor, Revenue Minister, is a Nehruite. Mr. S.S. Sharma, Chief Minister, is half Tandonite and half Nehruite. He voted for Tandon against Kripalani, for the Congress Presidency. Now he says "we cannot do without him [Nehru], the country cannot do without him." (978) A good acrobat. When Mr. Sharma remarks: "The Congress, after all, is the party of Gandhiji, the party of independence," (975) Mr. Kapoor, instead of contradicting his chief, almost in a soliloquy, thinks: "it was the party of good deal else besides: nepotism, corruption, inefficiency, complacency that Gandhiji himself had wanted it dissolved as a political force after independence." (975) He had, rightly, diagnosed the Nehruvian age and its difference from the Gandhian age. Mr. Sharma, a traditionalist, hitched himself to Nehru, grasping the truth that Nehru had future. Mr. Agarwal, a Tandonite (or, Patelite), holds a contrary opinion on Nehru and his indispensability for the nation and the party. When Mr. Sharma reminds him of Nehru's charm and indispensability he explodes: "Panditji—Panditji—why should everyone go on whimpering and pleading for everything to Nehru? Yes, he is great leader—but are there no other great leaders in Congress? Does Prasad not exist? Does Pant not exist? Did Patel not exist?" (978) Nehru is as much hungry for power as Tandon and Agarwal. The only difference is that Nehru represents the anglicized Indians and Tandon, the traditionalists. Ideology is a veneer for political gain. Nobody has the strength of character to die for his conviction. After a bout of political fight with Nehru for Congress Presidency, Tandon accepts the membership of the Congress Working Committee. Nehru, in the name of 'ism,' is out to wrest the seat of power from his formidable opponent, Tandon. Politics of the Gandhi age is accorded a state funeral.

Political corruption is also the abuse of power. A delegation of ten students (Rasheed among them) went to see the Home Minister. He refused to concede their demands. Nor did he budge an inch from his stated stance that he would maintain order in the town at any cost.

> "Does that mean you will shoot us if we get out of hand?" asked Rasheed with a malignant look.
>
> "I would prefer not to," said the Home Minister, as if the idea was not entirely unpleasant, "but, needless to say, it will not come to that." At any rate, he added to himself, the legislature is not presently in session to talk about it.
>
> "This is like the day of the British," continued Rasheed furiously, staring at the man who had justified police firing in Chowk, and perhaps seeing embodied in him the image of other arbitrariness and authoritarianism. (816)

The man, who opposed tooth and nail the policy brutalities in the British Raj then waxed eloquent on the inevitability of a lathi charge on students, at Brahmpur. The shift from direct speech to indirect speech, "At any rate, he added to himself, the legislature is not presently in session to talk about it," conjures up Agarwal's happy and fearful response to Rasheed's query. Agarwal had arrogated to himself the power of the Chief Minister (who is away in New Delhi) and the State Legislature is not in session "to talk about it." To him, the Assembly is a "talking shop," a name Carlyle gave about a hundred and fortyfive years ago to the British Parliament. But he also knows that this "talking shop" sometimes turns into a "gas chamber," in the words of Prof. Hiren Mukherjee. "I would state that in every form of government, whether autocratic or democratic, there is, over time, a progressive alienation of the governors from the governed. For a government has two objectives: to govern successfully and to preserve itself in power." Ten days after the assassination of Gandhi, Rajaji spoke from Calcutta: "Suppression and State coercion cannot be avoided in this imperfect world." Mr. Agarwal, like Julius Caesar, mutatis mutandis, can boast:

> I am constant as the northern star,
> Of whose true-fix'd and resting quality
> There is no fellow in the firmanent. (*Julius Caesar*, III, i, 60-2)

Ordinary men, Julius Caesar, boasts:

> are flesh and blood and apprehensive
> Yet in the number I do know but one
> That unassailable holds on this rank
> Unshak'd of motion, and that I am he.   (III, i, 67-70)

Mr. Agarwal had "enjoyed the power that went along with being Home Minister, and he knew that it was not a portfolio that could be given to anyone else, especially now that it was an open secret that Mahesh Kapoor was about to announce his resignation from the Congress party and the government." (822) Salisbury describes Disraeli as "a grain of dirt clogging the political machine." Mr. Agarwal can be described as a grain of dirt clogging the Indian political machine. But this is not entirely his fault. As discussed above, like William Godwin's Falkland, he can be seen as a warning against political system, in the immediate post-independence India, which enables him to become a tyrant. Audaces fortune juvat (fortune favours the bold). Fortune, in Hindi, is Lakshmi, Seth rightly calls Agarwal, Lakshmi Narayan Agarwal. On the contrary, 'Mahesh' is associated with Lord Shiva, amicus humani generis. So, Mahesh Kapoor is indifferent to Lakshmi, or even hostile. Power has a built-in element which may corrupt its possessor. Compared with the revolutionary promises of the pre-independence era with the accomplishments of the 1947-52 by Nehru one can say that power corrupts. But there are many men who want neither to enlarge their power nor to perpetuate it. One such man is Mr. Mahesh Kapoor, Revenue Minister of Purva Pradesh. He is a perfect match and a perfect contrast to Nehru. He piloted the Zamindari Abolition Bill in the Legislative Assembly, sacrified his friendship with the nawab sahib "for the greater good of millions of tenant farmers," (264) starched "his delicately embroidered kurtas into rigidity," and sacrificed his family happiness for the sake of his state. Gibbon, in *The Decline and Fall of the Roman Empire*, speaks of the united reigns of Antoninus Pius and Marcus Aurelius, "possibly the only period of history in which happiness of a great people was the sole object of government." Seth in *A Suitable Boy*, speaks of Mahesh Kapoor's work as Revenue Minister of Purva Pradesh as the only period in the early fifties in Indian history of 51-52 in which the happiness of a great people was the sole object of government. To stretch the analogy further, if Kapoor is Marcus Aurelius, then Agarwal is Commodus, a man in whom "every sentiment of virtue and humanity was extinct." Mr. Kapoor is not a son of Moloch, he is a Son of Aurelius. When offered a wad of money to soften a provision of the Zamindari Abolition Bill by the ruler of Marh, "I was tempted to have him arrested—title or no title." (326) On secularism, he says: "The basic problem is how the two religions will get on with each other in Brahmpur." (326) He further says: "I have a secular image—and in a town like this where everyone is beating the drum of religion, I am not going to join in with the shehnai. Anyway, I don't believe in this chanting and hypocrisy—and all this fasting by saffron-clad heroes who want to ban cow slaughter and revive the Somnath Temple and the Shiva Temple and God knows what else." (329) When the political tussle between the Tandonites and the Nehruites had become hot at Patna, he said to his wife: "'The Congress is threatening to split down the middle, people are defecting left and right to this party.' He stopped, then continued with increasing emotion: 'Everyone who is decent is leaving. . . . They are accusing us, rightly enough, of corruption, nepotism, and jobbery. . . . And your own husband feels much the same' he continued. 'This is not why I spent years of my life in prison. I am sick of the Congress Party, and I too am thinking of leaving it.'" (753)

There may be same truth in the 17th century British thinker Lord Halifax's view that "State business is a cruel trade and good nature is a bungler in it." First of all, he had resigned from the Congress Party and, therefore, lost his ministerial berth. Then, he had joined the KMPP, led by Kripalani. Again, he rejoined the Congress Party. "The power-seekers shrewdly ferret out the hid-

A Political Analysis 41

den points of vulnerability in their rivals, and work them over with the same impersonal cruelty as the prize fighter in the ring aiming his blows at his adversary's bleeding eyes. They dissimulate. They develop sudden public cravings for strawberries. They stage elaborate little theatrical in which, appropriately costumed, they themselves perform in a bid to manipulate opinion."[9] The resignation of Mahesh Kapoor from the Congress Party and his son Maan's involvement with Saeeda Bai and his attack on nawab sahib's son, Firoz, were some points of vulnerability which his opponents used, with cruelty, against Mahesh Kapoor when he, once again, was contesting the Assembly seat from the Congress Party. His main rival, Waris, is crude. "Waris had been appalled by Nehru's remarks about his master [nawab sahib], whom he revered.... He was not excessively nice about his methods."

On the day before the election, when it would be too late for any effective refutation, appeared a small handbill in Urdu, printed in the thousands on flimsy pink paper. It carried a black border. It appeared to have no author. There was no printer's name at the bottom. It announced that Firoz had died the previous night.... The murderer even now walked the streets of Brahmpur, free on bail, free to strangle more helpless Muslim women and slaughter the flower of Muslim manhood." (1244)

This canard against Mahesh Kapoor was spread by his opponent, Waris, fearing that the secular speech of Nehru and the secular image of Kapoor, would force him to lick dust, in the election of 1952. The alleged death of Firoz at the hand of Maan was a "fatalflier" (1244) but the Muslim population, swayed by this fatal flier, had voted en masse for a communalist, Waris and, thereby, rejected a secularist, Kapoor. And the tragedy is that Kapoor, like Nehru, failed to see how men could be roused by something as metaphysical as religion.

He was an upright person, exuding humility and something like the aura of integrity which was there, never put on. So, Kapoor felt "ashamed to say one word to inflame anyone on the grounds of religion." (1283) His sang-froid would not allow him even to submit an election petition to the Election Commission against the Salimpur result. Waris wills the means as well as the end. So does Shakespeare's Richard III and Lady Macbeth.

Shakespeare's Coriolanus is destroyed not because he is corrupt but because he has failed to come to terms with the forces of corruption. Seth's Kapoor is destroyed politically not because he is corrupt and communalist but because he has failed to come to terms with the forces of corruption. Or, I recall that in Athens of the 5th century B.C. a truly virtuous man Aristides, called "The Just" by almost everybody, was once "ostracized" that is to say, exiled by the citizens of that wonder city of old, because they were bored stiff with good man being praised so constantly! Kapoor's electorate and Seth exile Kapoor from the political scene, temporarily, because he is too good.

The mention of Kidwai leads me to the soliloquy of Mahesh Kapoor, in the house of nawab sahib, pinpointing Kidwai as "something of a river-dolphin. He enjoyed swimming in silty water and outwitting the crocodiles around him." (995) This accurate reading of Kidwai has political and monetary aspects, both. Madhu Limaye says: "Kidwai was a warm-hearted, outgoing personality. He had friends in all parties. Kidwai had an obliging nature, but I doubt whether he was scrupulous in the choice of his means. He revealed in intrigue and manipulative polities."[10] "To be honest as this world goes," says Hamlet to Polonius, "is to be one man pick out of ten thousand." At least, Kidwai was not that man. Mahesh Kapoor says of him: "Rafi Sahib, with his usual circus skills, is attending the meetings of both parties—and has got himself elected to the board of this new thing, this KMPP, this Peasants' and Workers' Party!" (753) He resigned both "from the Cabinet as Minister of Communications and the Congress Party." (956) The next day he announced the withdrawal of his resignation. Again, he was forced to resign. He had no qualms in dividing the party in the name of ideology and policy. The sordidness of this drama reminds one of Maria Theresa of Austria shedding tears over the first partition of Poland (1772) as the strangulation of a people. But, Frederick II of Prussia twitted her, "elle pleurait mais elle tenait" ("she wept but she took her share of Poland")! Kidwai was in many respects an alterego of Robert Cecil, James I's minister, a corrupt man, who climbed to power by devious means:

> God knows, my son,
> By what by-paths and indirect crook'd ways
> I met this crown.   (*Henry IV*, Part II, IV, v, 184-6)

L.N. Agarwal is as good a manipulator and devious as Cecil and Kidwai are, Kapoor says to his wife: "Agarwal is in Patna, Yes, Agarwal, Agarwal, who should be clearing up the Pus Mela mess, he's in Patna, manoeuvring endlessly, giving as much support to Tandon and as much trouble to Nehru as he possibly can." (753) Agarwal hails from the trading community and the caste consciousness never deserts him. Though he was the Home Minister of Purva Pradesh, he had never forgotten to cultivate his constituency which was populated by his caste-men. At one time in the novel, some jatavs picketed before the shopkeepers in Misri Mandi. A part of Misri Mandi lay in his assembly constituency. Agarwal was in dilemma. "They [jatavs] had doubtless been stirred up by union leaders.... Many traders there were already in financial straits. The threatened picketing would finish them off. L.N. Agarwal himself came from a shopkeeping family and some of the traders were good friends of his. Others supplied him with election funds. He had received three desperate calls from them.... It was not merely a question of law, but of order, the order of society itself." (230-31) "All virtues are directed towards self interest as river flow to sea," Rochefoucauld writes. For this self interest, Agarwal sacrificed the law of the land and had ordered the young District Magistrate to fire if the crowd did not disperse, to maintain order. The District Magistrate had suggested him an alternative to solve the problem of picketing but the Son of Moloch overruled the Son of Belial because it was the puppies of the ilk of Krishan Dayal (District Magistrate) who used to lock him up in British jails. (231) Agarwal, Kidwai and Cecil are corrupt, but paripassue, they are patriots to their finger-tips, also. One need not be a seventeenth century or Gandhian Puritan to know that the road to the celestial city lay through a lusty mart.

Jha, an old jack-in-the-box politician and friend of the Chief Minister and the Chairman of the Upper House of the state legislature "gets a large part of his funds from the landlord," (960) the same landlord against whom his party had slapped the Zamindari

Abolition Act. He believes, like a practical and matter of fact breed of politicians, that party and government are "two bullocks of one yoke," (963) and this sane advice of Jha to Sandeep Lahiri (S.D.O.) is yoked with the Congress election symbol (two bullocks yoked together) by Vikram Seth to highlight the principles and actions of Congressmen, in the early fifties. The party and the government being one, Jha asserted his right to order Lahiri to collect money for him. On his refusal to do so, Jha moved fast and got him transferred with "immediate effect from the post of Sub-Divisional Officer of Rudhia subdivision to a post in the Department of Mines at Brahmpur the same day." (969) Power is used to subvert the interest of the state and to gain his interest, by Jha. Once again the Son of Moloch defeats the Son of Belial.

Netaji, a Kidwai-in-making, is one more example of political corruption, for personal ends. "He had by now almost entirely forgiven Maan for his humiliation and successes had occurred since then, and on the whole he was making progress in his plans for world conquest." (674-75) The pawky neta knows that the pains and slings of humiliations are stones on the road to political exaltation. Supplication, flattery, self-interest and meanness are many steps of a ladder which will lead him to the top of political and material success. He, therefore, supplicated before Maan for a Kerosene dealer's licence, ingratiated before Lahiri to keep him in good humour, exhorted Rasheed and Maan to team up with him to get "things off their [old leaders'] feet," (620) and to take their place. The Sons of Belial, finding leaders of the nationalist movement tough, cringe before them but they make the younger generation cringe before them.

Various reasons can be given about why and how the political corruption, at first, seeped into our polity, and then, exuded, and finally has threatened to inundate it. First the "very leaders to whom power was transferred—(this was the phrase employed to describe the end of British rule, and that in itself is significant)— were incapable of doing anything positive. Till 1946 they had been mere agitators, and none of them cared to acquire ideas about what to do if the British went . . . the bankruptcy of ideas in the nationalist leaders was absolute, like the bankruptcy in business of a discharged bankrupt." When framing our constitution, the formulations, like in the French Declaration of the Rights of Man (1789) or the American Declaration of Independence (1776), about the people's right everywhere to "life, liberty and the pursuit of happiness" could not be made. Secondly, the secularism of the West, grafted on us, is not needed for "Hinduism as a religion is itself secular and it has sanctified worldliness by infusing it with moral and spiritual qualities."[12] The election, in 1952, rocks the secular boat of Mahesh Kapoor, of the Nehru brand and the Patelite brand of secularism, based on Dharma, helps Agarwal to sail smoothly on turbulent waters. For Kapoor this election is an elegy; for Agarwal it is a lyric.

Similarly, the western socialism endangered the indigenous genius of the people, bringing in its wake "Nehru's ideas of planned development, his fascination for big projects and a bureaucratic public sector, created a big and unwieldy government machine. . . . The controlled economy was tantamount to a licence-quota raj—Rajaji's picturesque phrase. The controls and the discretionary powers, which inevitably vested in the bureaucratic and political executive, gradually began to breed corruption and an ethos of permissiveness. First, the Congress began to collect funds for political purposes and for fighting elections. In the next stage the Ministers began to enrich themselves. The bureaucracy and the police took advantage of the vested powers."[13] Agarwal, Jha of the older group and Netaji of the younger group of politicians are the by-product of this 'ism.'

Panikkar observes, "Caste associations masquerade as political parties and caste groups function within political parties with distinct identities as pressure groups. The caste and communal divide in Indian society is well marked . . . and communal tensions and riots have become the order of the day."[14]

Then comes a new middle class. Sir Jadunath Sarkar observes, "Democracy cannot work without social equality and social equality has been conquered by this vast middle class moving across Hindu society like a steam roller. This non-official middle class has been the life and soul of our political agitation and supplied all its leaders."[15] After independence, people like Kapoor, Agarwal, Jha, belonging to this middle class, monopolize patriotism. Patient constructive workers for the nation's uplift are taunted with having made no sacrifice compared with the white-cap patriots. This attitude corresponds with the oratory of Agarwal on patriotism.

> "Yes, yes" said the Home Minister, cutting him short. "I know it. I lived through it. You must have been a boy of twelve then, watching anxiously in the mirror for the first signs of a man's hair. When you say 'us students' you don't mean yourselves, it was your predecessors whose blood was split. And, I may mention, some of mine." (817)

Patriotism of this type teaches a false sense of values to the electorate and encourages politicians to found bogus joint-stock banks.

Lastly, the extraordinary communion that Gandhi established with the masses of so-called "ordinary people," in Nehru remained superficial and tokenistic, as shown by the half-hearted nature of the Congress land reform in the years immediately after independence.

"How many of them," said Daisaku Ikeda, "however, could be truly said to be working on the side of the people and for their benefit. It is not going too far, I think, to say that the greater part of these leaders are in fact merely 'playing the crowd,' whom they secretly despise and whom they seek to use for their own purposes."[16] There is a riot in the Chowk killing "at least five people," (251) and a lathicharge in Misri Mandi. The "ordinary people," killed or lathi-charged, are not individuals, for politicians like Agarwal or Sharma or Kapoor. "What will the effect of all this be on the jatav vote and the Muslim vote? The General Elections are just a few months away. Will these vote-banks swing away from the Congress?" (242) Ram Dhan and Begum Abida Khan, raising these issues, as per their caste and religious denominations, convinced Agarwal that "this was indeed a plot by Muslims and so-called secular Hindus to attack him." (256) How callously the Home Minister tells his followers, "Either you rule, or you don't. The British knew that they had to make an example. ... Anyway, people are always dying—and I would prefer death by bullet to death by starvation." (260)

Can we prevent the further growth of the cancerous political corruption, in the present democratic set-up, in India? Vikram Seth has merely written about a period, 1951-52 and has neither exoticised nor criticized it. Therefore, the utter helplessness of an average India finds suitable expression in a piece of doggerel, written in the eighteenth century England. The popular rhyme ran thus:

> What this rogue loses, that rogue wins,
> All are birds of a feather!
> Let's damn the Outs, and damn the Ins.
> And damn them all together!

And, what our elected representatives think about it? A piece in *Newsweek* (3 February 1975), written on "Honourable Members" of British Parliament, finds an answer for them: "Virtually all MPs (in Britain) have to find ways of adding to their meagre 10,575 dollars a year salary, and lobbying happens to be a lucrative and easily come by way of keeping body and soul together. . . . The tradition that MPs are gentlemen and consequently incorrupt is akin to religious dogma in the mother of parliaments. When leftwing MP Joe Ashton recently charged that there were 'half a dozen MPs who are approachable. . . . You can hire their services and ask them to raise things in the House,' Ashton was promptly rapped over the knuckles by fellow-parliamentarians. "Members of the House," thundered Attorney General Samuel Silkin, "we are what we call one another—honourable members." The Indian politicians, in *A Suitable Boy*, are all honourable public servants, at least what they call one another. If *Hamlet* is a prologue to the drama of a corrupt polity, then, *A Suitable Boy* is its epilogue.

NOTES

1. S. Radhakrishnan, *Vision of India* (New Delhi: Indian Council for Cultural Relations, 1988), p. 175.
2. Ravindra Kumar quoted in Mark Tully and Zareer Masani's *From*

Raj to Rajiv (New Delhi: Universal Book Stall, 1989), p. 31.
3. Nirad C. Chaudhuri, "British Rule Is Dead, Long Live British Rule," *The Statesman* (Festivals), 1994, p. 8.
4. (Bombay: Jaico, 1969), p. 402.
5. "British Rule Is Dead," p. 10.
6. Moody E. Prior, *The Drama of Power: Studies in Shakespeare's History Plays* (Evanston, 1973), p. 144.
7. S. Schoenbaum, "*Richard II* and the Realities of Power," *Shakespeare Survey*, 1975, vol. 28, p. 10.
8. *Ibid.*
9. *Ibid.*, p. 13.
10. "Jawaharlal Nehru and Probity in Public Life," *The Statesman* (Festivals), 1994, p. 311.
11. "British Rule Is Dead," p. 10.
12. Nirad C. Chaudhuri, *Thy Hand, Great Anarch* (London: Chatto and Windus, 1987), p. 881.
13. Madhu Limaye, p. 311.
14. K.N. Panikkar, *Culture and Consciousness in Modern India* (New Delhi: People's Publishing House, 1990), p. 23.
15. *India through the Ages* (New Delhi: Sangam, 1979), p. 107.
16. "Towards a World without War . . ." (Gandhi Memorial Lecture 4) (New Delhi: Gandhi Smriti and Darshan Samiti, 1992), pp. 15-16.

The Chatterjees and Cuddles
Metaphor and Image in *A Suitable Boy*

F.R. Leavis, in his very early publication "Mass Civilization and Minority Culture," (1930) explained the role of the educated minority and their composition: "Upon this minority depends our power of profiting by the finest human experience of the past; they keep alive the subtlest and most perishable parts of tradition. Upon them depend the implicit standards that order the finer living of an age, the sense that this is worth more than that, this rather than that is the direction in which to go, that the centre is here rather than there."[1] From the very beginning Leavis places a tremendous burden on the minority; they alone, in effect, are responsible for, and can change, the health of modern society.

Granting that Leavis is concerned with more than a literary minority, his insistence on the crucial importance of the educated minority is in modern democratic society, frequently challenged or resisted. While the importance of the educated public may have been recognized in the nineteenth century of Coleridge and Arnold, in modern society the dominance of egalitarian ideas often leads to a straightforward rejection of the role of minorities. Leavis himself regards the prevalent hostility towards minorities, towards the educated public and thus to standards, as one of the sicknesses of contemporary society. William Walsh, in his essay on "The Literary Critic and the Education of an Elite," makes two observations that seem relevant to any egalitarian critique of minorities. First, Walsh notes that "Civilization, or 'culture' in Coleridge's and Arnold's sense, has always been the direct concern and the immediate product of minorities."[2] The importance of minorities in the past seems a fact, and there seems little reason to think that the situation has changed in the late twentieth century. Secondly, continuing his defence of minorities, Walsh argues: "Democracy has much to tell us about the equality of moral value of men but very little to say about the equality of intellectual capacity. And capacity, intellectual capacity, is to be the sole measure regulating the composition of the elite."[3]

The elite minority played a very significant role in India during the British rule. The British rule, though harmful in hundreds of ways, was the 'seed time of New India' rather than the dark age of modern India. First, Warren Hastings and Cornwallis helped the slow death of the old order. Second, the death of this order was a necessary process before the new order could come into being. To the English destroyer or the old order in India we may truly apply the words of the ancient Sanskrit poet Kalidas: "Holy father! this curse of yours is to me really a blessing in disguise. When the fire burns a cultivated field it makes it the more fertile for sending up shoots from the seeds sown."[4] In Lord Bentick's time, we find Indians again beginning to take an honourable and responsible part in guiding their countrymen's thoughts, shaping national life, and conducting the country's government. But these were Indians of a new breed; they drew their inspiration and their strength not from the East but from the West. They had acquired English learning and had thus properly equipped themselves for the work of the modern age. They were the first fruits of the Indian renaissance and their prophet was Raja Rammohan Roy, whose life (1744-1833) exactly bridges this dark age in the history of modern India.

Raja Rammohan Roy was the first Indian to write books in English and he visited England. Also, as early as 1789 we find an appeal by several Bengali gentlemen to Englishmen: "We humbly beseech any gentleman will be so good to us as to take the trouble of making a Bengali Grammar and Dictionary; in which we hope to find all the common Bengali country words made into English. By this means we shall be enabled to recommend ourselves to the English Government and understand their orders; this favour will be gratefully remembered by us and our posterity for ever?"[5]

Roy inherited mastery of Arabic and Persian from his forefathers; derived his grounding in Sanskrit literature and his familiarity with Hindu scriptures from his mother's forefathers, who were priests and pundits. Then, he acquired an effective command of English. By learning English, he could grasp the significance of modern and European philosophy, science and literature. It would be irrelevant to examine the details of the reforms initiated by Rammohan Roy, at this stage. What is relevant for us, in the present context, is to know something of a new religion, Brahmoism, founded by him. S.C. Sengupta writes about this new religion: "Only Rammohan and his followers would not agree with the Hindus that God could be worshipped in many forms and under many names. It seems that he had greater attraction for Unitarian Christianity than for Islam, which makes distinction between Allah and his prophet Mohammed. Rammohan thus made a noble and daring attempt at bringing together the various peoples of India by showing the spiritual affinity between the Upanishads, the Bible and the Quoran and also the Grantha-Sahib of the Sikhs. What exists is One; the sages call It by different names. This Upanishadic message was the kernel of his religion."[6] Its intellectual appeal, refined spirituality, and active social service brought many converts to it. The Chatterjees, in *A Suitable Boy*, are all Brahmos.

After Rammohan Roy, the greatest literary and social reformer was Bankim Chandra Chatterjee. For Rammohan Roy, the Upanishadic message is religious; for Chatterjee, there is only one God but this god is the motherland, the message of patriotism. The spiritual affinity of Bankim Chandra progresses to the very deification of the motherland, in which all other deities—Hindu, Muslim, Sikh, Parsee—merge themselves into one deity—Mother India. The conception and propagation of the idea of Mother India by Bankim Chandra Chatterjee led to the composition of the 'Bande Matram' hymn. Tagore's 'Jana-Gana-Mana' belongs to the Brahmo school of religion whereas Chatterjee's 'Bande Matram' is his own creation, unenumbered by any philosophy—ancient or modern. In Tagore and Chatterjee the influence of English literature is unmistakable, but equally unmistakable is their success in adapting the foreign spirit and literary model (and even technique) to the Indian mind and tradition. They represent the spirit of England clad in a half-oriental garb.

Sri Aurobindo was the fiery evangelist of Nationalism, the propounder of Integral Yoga, the prophet of the Life Divine, the interpreter of the Veda and, finally, a man of letters in excelsis, a master of prose art, and a dramatist and poet of great power and versatility. The politician, the poet, the philosopher, and the Yogi were all of a piece, and made the sum—the Power—that was Rishi Aurobindo. He turned the political movement in the country towards the right goal, and even determined somewhat the pace of its progress. He warned those leaders who were in favour of the partition of India into two nations that it was an act of lunacy. He was a mystic and Tagore vouchsafed it, after his meeting with him in his Ashram on 20 May 1928.

They were the 'elites,' in minority, who, steeped in European culture and literature, ordered the 'finer living of an age'—the modern age—in India. They had known that the centre of all political, social and cultural activities of modern India "is here rather than there." And their intellectual capacity "is to be the sole measure regulating" their composition.

Calcutta has always been in the vanguard of change in social, cultural, and political sphere. The English education, thus, produced a middle class, unknown in the history of India. We, in *A Suitable Boy*, are concerned with the anglicized upper middle-class Bengali element, mostly consisting of barristers and their families, living in old Ballygunje or the Chowringhee quarter. Nirad C. Chaudhuri describes them very accurately:

> They lived in aristocratic segregation, brought about in the first instance by the orthodoxy of the ordinary Bengali . . . and secondly by their own contempt for those whom they looked upon as the unredeemed rank and file of Bengali society. . . .
>
> There were no set of people better posted about the appropriate times and occasions for the different kinds of English clothes, and a wrong tie or hat was likely to give rise to more trouble among them than in the best English society. They called one of their streets Mayfair, and shunned all streets. . . . They preferred the European cuisine, although in its actual presentation by the Muslim bawarchis. . . . Their homes were provided with the usual drawing-rooms, dining-rooms, and studies.

Most of them had a highly literary culture, well-developed political sense, and awareness of social and political duties. . . . In family life, despite the fact that some affected the ways of the fast and more fell a prey to drink, the general tone was of Victorian respectability, strict discharge of family obligations, and steadiness. I use the adjective Victorian in a commendary sense, as I feel it should be.[7]

Calcutta was: Fuimus Troes, fuit Ilium.

It is but natural that Vikram Seth, writing on the intellectual-elite minority in India, in 1951-52, should choose Calcutta, like Tolstoy who chose St. Petersburg for his novel *War and Peace*. The English education arrived in Calcutta nearly a hundred years earlier than in Madras and much later in Delhi and other provincial cities. Therefore, the British Raj perpetuated itself longer in Calcutta in the persons who follow the Somerset Maugham ritual, and put on dinner-jackets and coats with ties. England's green and pleasant land has been washed up on Calcutta's Hooghly banks. Seth shows the elegance, the splash, and the grandeur of Calcutta. One more Vanity Fair, in which Byronism joins hands with dandyism to create a Victorian aura, detached from the group grievance of the rest of the people. Seth, like Thackeray, shows us a realistic account of the actual behaviour of men and women in upper-middle class Calcutta society of the early cities, reminiscent of John Bunyan's Vanity Fair in *Pilgrim's Progress*.

The Vanity Fair, in *A Suitable Boy*, consists of the Chatterjees, Arun Mehra and, of course, Cuddles. Heading the family is the old Chatterjee, a retired judge of Calcutta High Court, relishing the days of his retirement and also unmindful of the death of his wife, ten years after their marriage. He has unleashed the young judge Chatterjee on this self-contained world, of parties, fun and jokes. Justice Chatterjee, in turn, has unleashed "five children in strict alternation of sex: Amit, Meenakshi (who was married to Arun Mehra), Dipankar, Kakoli, and Tapan. None of them worked, but each had an occupation. Amit wrote poetry, Meenakshi played canasta, Dipankar sought the meaning of life, Kakoli kept the telephone busy, and Tapan, who was only twelve or thirteen, and by far the youngest, went to the prestigious boarding school, Jheel." (383-84)

Amit had studied Jurisprudence at Oxford but had not completed "his studies for the Bar at Lincoln's Inn, his father's old Inn." (384) Instead, he had received "a couple of university prizes for poetry," has written "some short fiction published here and there in literary magazines, and a book of poetry which had won him a prize in England." (384) Amit, I suggest, is Seth's half-brother sans Seth's instinct, like a trader's, for money. Seth a propos is an entrepreneur; Amit a badaud. Justice Chatterjee had unleashed him on this small world to bite all, who came into his contact, with his 'serious' poetry and the unborn novel.

Meenakshi was married to Arun Mehra who was neither "a Brahmo, nor of Brahmin stock, nor even a Bengali. . . . They (the Chatterjees) were only concerned that their daughter might not be able to afford the comforts of life that she had grown up with. But again, they had not swamped their married daughter with gifts." (385) She "bought her fortnightly stores—her white flour, her jam and Chivers Marmalade and Lyle's Golden Syrup . . . from Baboraltey, a couple of loaves of bread from a shop in Middleton Row ('The bread one gets from the market is so awful, Luts'), some salami from a cold store in Free School Street ('The salami from Keventers is dreadfully bland, I've decided never to go there again'), and half a dozen bottles of Beck's beer from Shaw brothers." (372) She would never miss her canasta. A perfect memshaib. She had been unleashed on Arun Mehra, a young man from a conservative society and family, the son of Mrs. Mehra, a traditionalist. She had illicit relations with Billy Irani. The bite of the Chatterjees has transmogrified him into their breed.

Dipankar was a dreamer. "He had studied economics, but spent most of his time reading about the poet and patriot Sri Aurobindo. . . . Dipankar was indecisive by nature. . . . Dipankar treated every decision like a spiritual crisis. Whether to have one spoon of sugar in his tea or two, whether to come down now or fifteen minutes later, whether to enjoy the good life of Ballygunje or to take up Sri Aurobindo's path of renunciation, all these decisions caused him endless agony." (386) He is always on a lookout for a prey. His permanent victim is Varun who "was a better listener than anyone in Dipankar's own family, who became impatient when he talked about the Skein of Nothingness or the Cessation of Desire." (444) "Dipankar, despite his mystical and religious tendencies, was fond of even foolish young women." (393) A psychotic case.

Kakoli "was deeply attached to the telephone, and monopolized it shamelessly—as she did the car. Often she would burble on for forty-five minutes on end," (405) "a really shameless girl." (411) She "suffered her share of heartbreak," (448) but she had found out Hans, a German, as her latest companion and fan. She had loved singing Chopin but "now that she was accompanying Han's singing she had grown to like Schubert more and more." (499) An Indian Lydia, she had flirted with many society boys till she landed in the lap of Hans. Her obsession with phone and good society is almost psychotic.

Tapan "was the baby of the family whom everyone loved and fussed over, and who was even allowed an occasional sip of sherry himself." (386) He was the baby sahib. A student of Jheel, he would like to be admitted in St. Xavier's School, Calcutta. He, like Kakoli, was a composer of doggerels.

Justice Chatterjee, though small in size, short-sighted, and fairly absent-minded, was a man of some dignity: "He inspired respect in court and a sort of obedience even in his eccentric family. He didn't like to talk more than was necessary." (407) His well-developed political sense could not abide "the denigration of all things British or tainted with 'pseudo-British liberalism'; and resentment bordering on contempt for the sly milksop Gandhi who had dispossessed Bose of the presidentship of the Congress party which he had won by election many years before . . . but he—like his father, 'old Mr. Chatterjee'—was profoundly grateful that the likes of Subhas Bose had never succeeded in ruling the country." (467) A characteristic anglicized Bengali elite, soaked in everything English, a lapdog of British imperialism.

Mrs. Chatterjee is a perfect match to Mr. Chatterjee. She says: "And democracy is half our trouble. And that's why we have all these disorders and all this bloodshed." (398) She is also a perfect contrast to Mr. Chatterjee. Her deification of Sri Rabindranath Tagore—his poetry and Sangeet—her search for a suitable boy for Kakoli and her dislike for people, belonging to lower strata of society, is a part of her mental make-up.

The Chatterjee mansion is "such a zoo." In Angus Wilson's novel *The Old Men at the Zoo*, the novelist shows us political wrangling at the London Zoo—how it shall be run, what its future shall be. It is a small enclosed world, but it is an integral part of British culture. Similarly, the Chatterjee mansion is a small enclosed world—a world of the anglicized brown sahibs—but is an integral part of Indian culture. Mrs. Chatterjee is a great admirer of Tagore and Bengali. Mr. Chatterjee and his children often use Bengali clothes and language. Their mansion is a "scene of cordial conflict," (407) Mr. Chatterjee listens to Mr. Ganguly for a while with "amiable disgust," (466) examples of oxymoron. The usual reserve, restraint and dignity of an anglicized class is often broken by the eccentric children whom he (Mr. Chatterjee) is "in fact quite fond of." (466) 'Zoo' is a metaphor for the small enclosed world of the Chatterjees.

The Chatterjees, like the residual-claimants of British culture, host parties at home to entertain friends and relatives. This reminds me of an evening reception or, soiree given by a society lady in St. Petersburg, in July 1805, in Tolstoy's *War and Peace*. The talk about Napoleon is mingled with gossip and the affected courtesies exchanged in high society. We get to know various individuals. None of them seems very remarkable, though there are clear differences between them. A picture of the aristocratic life of these days is brought before our eyes. The soiree at the Chatterjee mansion is held in 1951, four years after our independence. But the atmosphere and the people are the same aristocrats and snobs that we find in *War and Peace*: "the women fluttering and flattering and sizing each other up, the men engaging themselves in more self-important chatter. British and Indian, Bengali and non-Bengali, old and middle-aged and young, saris shimmering and necklaces glimmering." (388) Ila Chattopadhyay is brute to the point of ridicule; Mr. Kohli, a very sound teacher of Physics, is a chatter-box; Hans is so polite and courteous that "courtesy is something of a disease" to him and so on. Mr. Kohli and Mrs. Chatterjee castigate democracy and the "middle-aged, accusing-looking woman with large, popping eyes" (389) writes a poem without a rhyme, in a hospital, after being bitten by mosquitoes.

Cuddles is an image for the Chatterjees, their ways of life, their manners, moods and modes of living:

> Cuddles was not a hospitable dog. He had been with the Chatterjee family for more than ten years, during which time he had bitten Biswas Babu, several school children (friends who had come to play), a number of lawyers (who had visited Mr. Chatterjee's chambers for conferences during his years as a barrister), a middle-level executive, a doctor on a house call, and the standard mixture of postmen and electricians. (387)
>
> Amit reflected that Cuddles was the most psychotic lapdog he had known. (388)

A lapdog is an image of prestige for every elite irrespective of clime and country. In one of his famous short stories entitled "The Chameleon," Anton Chekhov writes about a lapdog of an aristocrat, in the nineteenth century Russia, who has bitten a poor man. The poor man complains to the police against the dog and demands compensation from its owner. Instead, he gets foul abuse and dirty looks from the police. In the tradition of Chekhov, Seth allows Cuddles to bite people who come to the mansion of Mr. Chatterjee. As stated above, Cuddles is an image for the Chatterjees and the Chatterjees, individually, have bitten more people like Cuddles, and unlike the dog of Chekhov's story. The image extends beyond this bite to a generalization—a lapdog is also an image of servility. Now, this generalization about servility is linked with a disease called psychosis. This psychosis had assumed the form of an epidemic, called phorenophilia, in Seth's *A Suitable Boy*. Panikkar very aptly describes it:

> They [the aristocrat middle class] conversed in the morning like English gentlemen about possible changes in weather, in a country where weather hardly experienced any fluctuation for months together, wore double breasted suit and tie in hot and sultry Indian summers and learnt to waltz and trot in dancing halls. Their social prestige was measured in terms of

the number of invitations to the Governor's banquets and to the tea parties and dinners hosted by lesser English officials. More importantly, their intellectual perspectives were directed at the Metropolis. Admission to prestigious schools in England was highly sought after and a degree from either Oxford or Cambridge became the ultimate in intellectual attainment. Regardless of their intellectual ability, they returned to India to occupy positions of power and prestige.[8]

The Chatterjees have employed two cooks, one for Bengali and one for western food. The "Mugh cook, who came from Chittagong and excelled in European food, was dispatched to Sunny Park within the half hour." (373) In Sunny Park, Arun and his wife lived. Arun had invited Basil Cox and his wife of Bentsen & Pryce to dinner. Arun is a pucca brown sahib. So is Meenakshi. But his brother Varun is not plagued by phorenophilia, "He had once, in a fit of anti-imperialism and xenophobia, scrawled 'Pug' on two Bibles at St. George's School. . . . Arun too had bawled him out after this incident." (378) In contrast to Arun, Varun is a traditionalist: "Varun looked at him shiftily, 'What's embarrassing about Indian clothes?' he asked. 'Can't I wear what I want to? Ma and Lata and Meenakshi Bhabhi wear saris, not dresses. Or do I have to keep imitating the whiteys even in my own house?" (379) Amit had studied at Oxford, had become a poet and wastrel but was of no use to his parents and to his society itself. Dipankar was an Aurobindoite but ended up as an employee in a foreign bank. Meenakshi played canasta, had lost her cultural moorings and flirted with Billy Irani, even after her marriage. Kakoli sang Chopin and when she picked up Hans, the German nutcracker, she had begun to tune in with him with Schubert: "Once the process of intellectual colonization for an individual is contemplated," says Joon-Chien, "it acts a powerful control over him and guides his thoughts, and not infrequently, his actions, too. The value and ideals implanted during the process of intellectual colonization become so natural a part of him that as a mentally subjected individual, he is not only happy, contented and proud of them but very often he becomes their ardent defender and propagator."[9]

Metaphor and Image

"Cuddles was not a hospitable dog," (387) and neither were the Chatterjees. Mrs. Mehra found their hospitality nauseating, stifling and disgusting. They always giggled, philosophized, rhymed and mimed. She was afraid lest her daughter Lata contract this disease of phorenophilia. Mercifully, Lata was immune to this disease, though she enjoyed their company. Varun had found his brother's house quite inhospitable with all foreign paraphernalia—table manners, English dress and insufferable Arun and Meenakshi. Only Biswas Babu fitted into the Chatterjee mansion, like Cuddles. This is all happening in 1951-52, four or five years after our independence. "When we became politically free," says Mahadevan, "nearly three decades ago, who the hell coaxed and cajoled us to hang on to Macaulay's coat-tails? No one except our own pussilanimous, pettifogging, priggish prima donnas—our so-called founding fathers! Most of them had their roots in the muddle-headed, cocksure, plagiaristic climate of ideas that was characteristic of the Victorian era. . . . In short . . . our dear land, at a turning-point in its history, fell into the hands of epigones."[10]

'Psychosis' is a mental derangement, especially when resulting in delusions and loss of contact with external reality. Lata asks Amit:

> "How far have you got so far with writing it (novel)?" she said.
> "I'm about a third of the way."
> "And aren't I wasting your time?"
> "No."
> "It's about the Bengal Famine, isn't it?"
> "Yes."
> "Do you have any memory of the famine yourself?"
> "I do. I remember it only too well. It was only eight years ago." He paused, "I was somewhat active in student politics then. But do you know, we had a dog even then, and fed it well."
> He looked distressed. (484)

Is it not delusion that Amit writes about the Bengal Famine, admitting that they had fed their dog well? Is he not doing injustice to his writing? I guess Amit would be doing a lot of research on the Famine, like Seth who did a lot of research to write *A Suitable Boy*. This is a cinch—and I am willing to wager my last shirt on it.

Dipankar suffers from another delusion. He is probing the root of the nothingness in a house which has everything and the cessation of desire when he is fond of even foolish young women. Mr. Ganguly praises Fascism because Hitler helped Subhas Chandra Bose. The old Chatterjee read old plays because "King, princess, maidservant—whatever they thought then is still true now. Birth, awareness, love, ambition, hate, death, all the same." (467) For Arun, the British and not Indians, Americans and the Reds represent Freedom, Democracy, Humanity and Culture. But Jock Mackay, an Englishman, is not under any delusion nor cut off from reality: "'But it's a charming country on the whole,' he continued expansively. 'By the end of the Raj they were so busy slitting each other's throats that they left ours unslit. Lucky.' He sipped his drink." (402)

Admirers of Vikram Seth tend to compare *A Suitable Boy* with *War and Peace*. Tolstoy's elites grow whereas Seth's don't. Seth's elites, unlike Tolstoy's are not united in their search for spiritual truth. Tolstoy's elites cannot be happy unless they acquire some insight into the meaning of life and human destiny. They cannot be reconciled to the trivialities of daily existence unless they can catch some glimpse of the power that rules over all. This spiritual awakening comes to them in different ways and can never be forced. They are seekers, but however hard they seek, the moment of enlightenment will choose its own time. But to them, Tolstoy's elite, that enlightenment is essential. They cannot really live without it, and to all such people, today as in his own time, his message seems to be: "Seek, and ye shall find." Seth makes Veena sing Gandhi's favourite hymn, 'Uth, Jaag musafir.' Immediately after this hymn was sung, Mahesh Kapoor reflects: "The song ... brought home to him like nothing else had his unrealized loss. Gandhi was dead, and with him his ideals." (1225) Tolstoy's Prince Andrews is intellectually and culturally capable of leading the majority. Seth's elites can be described vividly in following lines:

Come, Heart, we have been handed our passports,
Love's visa has expired
The consulate of Truth is closed
And virtue's signature is no longer valid.[11]

Cuddles is the image of the loyalty, and servility, sexual frustration, ferocity, timidness, frivolity, and self-delusion. Their phorenophilia, stripped to the bone, is but a species of dishonesty. All the young Chatterjees are the saliva brothers and sisters of Cuddles. The Chatterjees, unlike Prince Andrews, Rammohan Roy and Bankim Chandra, are incapable of leading the majority. They are dolls and fakes. Vikram Seth is to Leo Tolstoy what Ben Jonson was to William Shakespeare.

NOTES

1. F.R. Leavis, *For Continuity* (Cambridge: The Minority Press, 1933), p. 15.
2. William Walsh, *The Use of Imagination* (Harmondsworth: Penguin, 1966), p. 72.
3. *Ibid.*, p. 76.
4. Kalidas, *Raghuvamsam*, IX, p. 80.
5. *Selections from the Calcutta Gazette*, 23 April 1789, ii, p. 497.
6. S.C. Sengupta, *Swami Vivekananda and Indian Nationalism* (Calcutta: Sahitya Samsad, 1984), p. 8.
7. Nirad C. Chaudhuri, *An Autobiography of an Unknown Indian* (Bombay: Jaico, 1969), pp. 403-4.
8. K.N. Panikkar, *Culture and Consciousness in Modern India* (New Delhi: People's Publishing House, 1990), pp. 33-34.
9. Doh Joon-Chien, *Eastern Intellectuals and Western Solutions* (New Delhi: Vikas, 1980), p. 10.
10. T.K. Mahadevan, *Ideas and Variations* (New Delhi: Mittal, 1988), p. 75.
11. Cyril Connolly, *The Condemned Playground* (London: The Hogarth Press, 1985), p. 279.

The Multiple Plot in *A Suitable Boy*

Referring to the plot of *Tom Jones* Dudden has observed:

> *Tom Jones* . . . is a classic example of a perfectly coherent story, most carefully planned from the very beginning, progressing slowly but surely through a succession of strictly relevant characters and events, and terminating in a logically appropriate catastrophe. No doubt it was mainly on account of his superb constructive art that Scott bestowed on Fielding the honourable title of 'Father of the English Novel.'
>
> The unity of *Tom Jones* is not secured by mere limitation of the subject matter. The book is a large, full, complex book, abounding in incidents and characters. There is certainly nothing meagre or contracted about it. The unity of the whole is achieved solely by means of a severe subordination of all the multitudinous details to the central plan. In the long and elaborate history hardly anything is found which does not in some way or other contribute to carry forward the main action to its conclusion.

In a novel, the preference is for "real life and manners," and Fielding portrays them abundantly with an exception in favour of 'ghosts.' Scott, his junior in this field, takes up historical characters and events in *The Heart of Midlothian*. But as G.P. Gooch remarked in 1945 in his lecture before the Royal Society of Literature, "what might have been is not the same thing than what was." Luckily, Scott relied more on his invented people and incidents than on actual historical personages and events and, thus, paved the way for future novelists like Dumas, Thackeray and Dickens to write *The Three Musketeers, Henry Esmond* and *A Tale of Two Cities*, respectively.

A novel, to be a work of art, needs unity: and unity in a novel involves the imposition of the logic of 'plot' on the material of the 'story.' In E.M. Forster's words, "a plot is also a narrative of events, the emphasis falling on causality . . . the time-sequence is preserved, but the sense of causality overshadows it." The imposition of causality is possible only in relation to the invented characters and situations. With the historical events and people, the novelist is in bondage to the known facts, and hence the novelist is not at liberty to impose his own logic on the events. In Thackeray's *Henry Esmond*, it is the human drama involving the destinies of Esmond and Lady Castlewood that holds the centre, the rest—including the Anglo-French wars and the literary ardours of Addison and Steele—being little more than elements in a decorative framework. In Tolstoy's *War and Peace*, while Alexander, Napoleon and Kutuzov hover as it were in the background, our main gaze follows the fortunes of the invented characters—Pierre, Natasha, Audrey and the rest.

It is significant that Tolstoy divides his novels into parts, thus showing a consciousness of larger groupings of material than is indicated by the chapter division. The principle is—given his three main centres of interest (Anna, Vronsky, Levin), or his six main characters, one of whom is present throughout and dominant—to carry them forward chronologically through eight main periods, or phases, massing the experience of each group or centre during the limited period of time. Generally each part will be confined to the events of three months—summer, winter or spring.

In George Eliot's *Middlemarch* there is no central figure of any kind; the main interest is divided between four separate groups of characters; and none of these except Dorothea Brooke approaches the conventional heroic type.

In Vikram Seth's *A Suitable Boy* the main interest is divided between four families—the Mehras, the Chatterjees, the Kapoors and the Khans—and only two—Lata and Maan—approach the conventional heroic types. Each family has a plot and therefore, there are four plots and there are some sub-plots here to help the four plots to advance slowly and steadily towards the main plot— the search for a suitable boy. The sub-plots—the academic skullduggery, the political parallellism between Nehru and Tandon, on the one hand, and, the political rift between L.N. Agarwal and Mahesh Kapoor, on the other, Saeeda Bai and Maan, all help the main plot to stand on surer and firmer footing.

The Mehras are led by Mrs. Rupa Mehra (visibly) and Late Raghubir Mehra (invisibly). Lata, Savita and Pran (son of Mahesh Kapoor and son-in-law of Mrs. Mehra), Varun are on the side of Mrs. Mehra and, therefore, are traditionalists. Arun Mehra and his wife, Meenakshi Mehra (daughter of Justice Chatterjee) represent modernity.

The Chatterjees are led by Justice Chatterjee, judge of Calcutta High Court and his father, a retired judge of Calcutta High School, five children and Mrs. Chatterjee are his protege. All, some ways or other, are snobs and symbolize the twilight glory of the British Raj and culture. But Dipankar, in spite of being a Chatterjee, is an Aurobindoite; Mrs Chatterjee, a worshipper of Rabindranath Tagore.

The Kapoor clan is headed by Mr. Mahesh Kapoor, Revenue Minister in the S.S. Sharma ministry of Purva Pradesh, a Nehruite. His wife, Mrs. Kapoor, is deeply religious, superstitious and conservative. His daughter Veena is married into the Tandon family, with Kedarnath Tandon. His elder son Pran Kapoor, an asthmatic lecturer in English at Brahmpur University, is married into the Mehra family, with Savita Kapoor. With the exception of Mahesh Kapoor and Maan Kapoor, the family is, on the whole, traditionalist.

The Khan clan is headed by the old Nawab Sahib of Baitar, an old aristocrat, a big landlord and a big man, in all respects. His sons Imtiaz Khan and Firoz Khan and his daughter Zainab are all birds, sitting on the Khan tree, singing in their own individual tone. Only Begum Abida Khan is the most aggressive, modern and feudal.

All these four plots, outlined briefly, are supported by the subplots of lesser dimensions, lesser importance, but equally run along with the four plots. The sub-plot of the academic skullduggery is managed by Prof. Mishra, Head, Dept. of English, Brahmpur University, supported by his traditional allies, the teachers, with the exception of Pran Kapoor. He is as much a

The Multiple Plot

traditionalist in the academic field as L.N. Agarwal is in politics.

The sub-plot of L.N. Agarwal, pitted against Mahesh Kapoor, helps to highlight the political rivalry of the warring groups in India in 1951-52, between the Nehruites and the Tandonites. Mr. L.N. Agarwal is a traditionalist, in the group of Sri Purusottomdas Tandon; Mr. Mahesh Kapoor, a progressive secularist, is a follower of Nehru.

The tannery work of Haresh is another sub-plot, running along with Mrs. Mehra, Mr. Mishra, Mr. Agarwal and Mrs. Kapoor. Haresh is a no-nonsensical businessman, like the Tandons, and unlike the Chatterjees and the Khans.

A Suitable Boy, in his elephantine size and movement, carrying on it so many plots and sub-plots, moves slowly and painfully, halts, at some places for digressions, like *Vanity Fair* of Thackeray or *Middlemarch* of George Eliot, and unlike *War and Peace*.

Of the plot of *Vanity Fair* Legouis and Cazamian write very aptly: "At first the plot unfolds itself very logically, emanates, so to speak, from the characters themselves; but, when a hundred and one providential happenings intervene, it very soon loses its firm outline. On the whole it is so long and complicated, so mingled with extraneous elements—in the present case entire episodes borrowed from recent history—the trend of thought is interrupted by so many digressions and moral reflections, that the work when viewed at one glance, seems very loosely put together." If we apply this criticism on *A Suitable Boy*, it fits into the plot, wonderfully. The novel starts, like *Pride and Prejudice*, in a dramatic method, full of dialogues, actions and unfolding of characters, like the unfolding of flowers in the morning. Mrs. Mehra is another Mrs. Bennett. Lata is Elizabeth Bennett and the marriage of her sister Savita with Pran is in full swing, full of bonhomie and suspicion. Pran is the son of a minister and Savita is the daughter of a middling middle class Mrs. Mehra. Then, there is the meeting of S.S. Sharma, Chief Minister, Purva Pradesh with his senior colleague L.N. Agarwal and his old friend, Nawab Sahib, at the reception hosted at Prem Niwas, the residence of Mr. Kapoor. The stories of the Mehras and the Kapoors, held together by two plots, are, now meandering aimlessly and gets bogged down in the story of Prof. Mishra, a clever manipulator.

But Prof. Mishra foreshadows the clever manipulation of Mr. L.N. Agarwal.

The plot of the Chatterjees is concerned with mainly two or three characters—Amit, Dipankar and Meenakshi. Amit falls into love with a Mehra, Lata Mehra. Meenakshi is already married to Arun Mehra. So, these two characters of the Chatterjee plot are linked with the Mehra plot. But in one way, Dipankar's search for spiritual base in this mela of life is contrasted with the materialistic search for a suitable boy for Lata by Mrs. Rupa Mehra. The search of Dipankar finally lands him in the materialistic world, a job in Grindlay Bank.

The plot of the Nawab is concerned mainly with two characters—the Nawab Saheb and Firoz. The story of the Nawab Sahib is intertwined with Mahesh Kapoor, for they are very intimate friends and, in spite of the Zamindari Abolition Act, they remain spiritually good friends. Neither Mahesh Kapoor nor the Nawab likes to introduce dirty politics, to win election. Similarly, Firoz is an intimate friend of Maan. Though Maan fatally injures Firoz in a drunken state, Firoz absolves him of this charge, gladly.

By now it is clear that plots of *A Suitable Boy* are structured around pursuit or search and this gives force and coherence to the novel. Mrs. Mehra is in search of a suitable boy for Lata; Dipankar is in search for a spiritual base; Mr. Mahesh Kapoor is in search of a political base and the Nawab is in search of his feudal stability. All these searches are centred in the period of 1951-52, the period of newly-free country, embarking on the path of finding a permanent footing, internally and externally. India was searching within itself and outside itself. This historical search is interwoven with domestic searches and the novel assumes a socio-politico-historical form.

The main character in the political history of 1951-52 Pt. Jawaharlal Nehru and three fictional characters, S.S. Sharma, Mahesh Kapoor and L.N. Agarwal are props to enlarge the small presence of Nehru in the novel. What would be our India, externally and internally, is shown to us through the speech of Pt. Nehru at Baitar and his letters to Chief Ministers, periodically. We quote his speech at Baitar: "The world is going through a hard time. We have the Korean crisis and the crisis in the Persian Gulf.

The Multiple Plot

You have already heard about the attempt of the British to bully the Egyptians. . . . This is bad, and we cannot have it. The world must learn to live in peace." (1240) This speech amply foreshadows the policy of non-alignment that India propounded and followed in the years to come. Then we come to the second part of his speech: "Here at home also, we must live in peace. As tolerant people we must be tolerant. . . . Disaster will strike the country if religious bigots and communalists of all descriptions get their way." (1240) This part of his speech forms part of his habit to brief Chief Ministers on issues affecting India, internally and externally. We quote the letter of Pt. Nehru to Chief Ministers dated 9 August 1951:

> Sometimes it is said that there might be bad elements among the Muslims who might give trouble. . . .
> We must give full protection to our minorities. This means also that we must not permit any propaganda on the part of Hindu and Sikh communal organizations, which is on a par with Pakistan propaganda on the other side. (976-77)

Letters and speech of Pt. Nehru are a sort of quest or search and fictional characters—Sharma, Kapoor, Agarwal—are his answers. Sharma, once a Tandonite, is, in 1952, a Nehruite. Kapoor, unlike Nehru, fails to act swiftly or to pull off a coup, when confronted with situation created by Waris. He, therefore, loses the Assembly election, in 1952. Agarwal, though a Tandonite, is a politician in his true colour, knows when to pull off a coup and, therefore, succeeds Sharma. The quest of India for domestic and foreign policies ends with the victory of Pt. Nehru and his party in 1952. India will now be secular and non-aligned.

The search of India for a suitable place in the comity of nations is interwoven with the search of Mrs. Mehra for a suitable boy for Lata. The clash of the Tandonites and the Nehruites, the traditionalists and the progressives has its echo, in the minds of Mrs. Mehra and Lata, whether to choose progressives like Kabir or Amit or a traditionalist like Haresh. The defeat of Mahesh Kapoor at the Assembly election, the elevation of L.N. Agarwal to the seat of Chief Ministership of Purva Pradesh, the temporary truce between Tandon and Pt. Nehru finally wheels the choice of Mrs. Mehra and Lata around Haresh, educated in England but rooted in India—half-Nehru and half-Tandon.

Similarly, the search of Dipankar for a spiritual base, meandering through zigzag paths, through Aurobindo, through Sanaki Baba "who is a man of great wisdom and sweetness and humour ... so I have decided to find that ease, and I have also decided that the bank of the Ganga is the place where I will find it." (717) Prior to that, his "interests in mysticism were wide-ranging, and included Tantra and the worship of the Mother-Goddess besides the more conceptual 'synthetic' philosophy he had just been expounding.... Half an hour later it was Unity, Duality, and the Trinity, on which Dipankar had recently had a crash-course." (446) But in the camp of Sanaki Baba, and at Pul Mela, he has come to realize "that the spiritual source of India is not the Zero or Unity or Duality or even the Trinity, but Infinity itself." (717) This linear progression from Aurobindo to Sanaki Baba and from Sanaki Baba to a service in a foreign bank, is the quest of Dipankar for a place under the sun and he, like Lata, finds it not in spirituality but in a materialistic world of hurly-burly and money and, ironically in Economics.

The quest of the Nawab Sahib to save his lands from the draconian Zamindari Abolition Bill ends in fiasco and he, more and more, goes into the world of meditation, prayer, reflection and reconciliation. His reconciliation with Kapoor and the judgement of the Supreme Court upholding the validity of the Zamindari Acts come, coincidentally, within a few days of the release of Maan and the discovery of the nefarious role, played by Waris, in arousing communal feelings among Muslims against Mahesh Kapoor. The search of the Nawab Sahib is over. He has found who his well-wishers are and who his detractors are.

The sub-plot of the Pran-Mishra academic difference, has been written by Vikram Seth to link the family of Mahesh Kapoor with Mrs. Rupa Mehra, at first glance, but beneath this, there is that search—whether James Joyce should be put in the syllabus or not, whether Pran should be chosen as reader in the dept of English, Brahmpur University. Pran represents modernity and Prof.

The Multiple Plot 69

Mishra represents tradition. The main point—the clash between the Tandonites and the Nehruites—percolates, down to the academy also, symbolically. The selection of Pran for the readership and the choice of James Joyce for the syllabus is something of a victory for modernity but mind it, Prof. Mishra is very much there, hovering over the scene. Once again, the uneasy truce between the forces of modernity and tradition.

Like the ordinary Victorian plot full with the stories of strokes of fortunes, coincidence, sudden inheritance, long lost wills, the plot of *A Suitable Boy* takes recourse to one such stock-in-trade story, i.e. of Saeeda Bai. Saeeda Bai plays a very important role in this novel and we are also unaware that Tasneem was the daughter of the Nawab. The Nawab Sahib had been secretly sending financial help to her. All of a sudden, like a detective story, we discover that Tasneem is his illicit daughter. We go into the tumult of his mind: "He did not know what interpretation to place upon the rejection of his continuing financial help to Saeeda Bai. He was more troubled than relieved. He did not really think of Tasneem as his daughter, or feel any affection for this unseen being, but he did not want her to suffer. Nor did he wish Saeeda Bai now to feel free to publish to the world whatever it suited her convenience to publish. He begged God to forgive him for the unworthiness of this concern, but he was unable to put it aside." (1300) The second specimen confirms the blood relationship of the Nawab Sahib with Tasneem: "Tasneem, though she was no doubt his half sister, meant nothing to Imtiaz at all. Zainab, too, though she was curious, realized that wisdom lay in closing the door of interpretation." (1301) The second surprise, sprung on us by Seth, is that the "Banaras people had decided that Maan was no longer a suitable boy; they had informed Mahesh Kapoor of their decision." (1341) Throughout the novel, the Banaras people are mentioned but never shown in action. None of them has ever espied on Maan nor has anybody shown to report to them, directly. Suddenly, they send their refusal. It is something like the sudden death of Mrs. Wilcox in *Howards End*.

We have discussed in the beginning that it is only Lata and Maan who perform some heroic deeds. Lata chooses her husband with great aplomb, rejecting Durrani and Amit, which was not an easy task. Then, she is assaulted by her own mausha, Sahgal and she fights it out cleverly. She also mixes with the anglophile Chatterjees without losing her Indianness. Normally, she would have been ensnared by the glamour of the Chatterjees, like her brother Arun. Maan, the son of a Cabinet Minister, falling in love with a courtesan, Saeeda Bai, his visit to Rasheed and his family at Rudhia, his youthful and zealous campaign for his father, his imprisonment on account of his alleged kniving of Firoz and finally, his acquittal by the Court on the evidence of Firoz, makes him perform some heroic deeds.

Vikram Seth, unlike his predecessors in India, admits that "this novel is linear partly because it's multilinear. There are several plots in it."[1] Viney Kirpal writes of third world novels:

> There is, first of all, the loose, circular, episodic loop-like narrative technique of the third world novel that marks it off from the modern, western novel. Within this broad generalization, of course, one finds a number of variations. For example, Mulk Raj Anand uses the Indian fable and folktale form in *Untouchable* and *Two Leaves and a Bud*. Raja Rao in *Kanthapura*, Anantha Murthy in *Samskara* and Karanth in *Mookaji's Visions*, employ the Puranic, digressive way of story-telling. R.K. Narayan's novels show the influence of the *Panchatantra* and the epics, while Rushdie patterns *Midnight's Children* after the episodic, digressive mode of the *Ramayana*.[2]

All these novels are plotless in the western critical sense, that is, they lack formal logic. They are loosely-structured, circular, reverberative, and they do not follow the usual pattern of development and action in the western novel. Not so *A Suitable Boy*. Seth adopts neither the fable and folktale form nor the Puranic nor the epic and the *Panchatantra* nor the *Ramayana* form of narrative. The reason is obvious. Vikram Seth's great heroes "in the novel form are people like the Victorians or the Chinese novelist of *The Story of the Stone* or Tolstoy. So Jane Austen, Tolstoy, George Eliot, people like that."[3] *A Suitable Boy* has a linear plot, that is, it has a formal logic. Some digressions are there, for instance, the long history of the political feud between Tandon and Nehru, the debates of the P.P. Legislative Assembly, the incurable rhyming of the Chatterjees and the poetry citation at the Brahmpur literary society. But the central strand of the book, the matrimonial quest of Mrs. Rupa Mehra is connected with the quest of so many characters, their lifestyles and mindsets. It is also the quest of Vikram Seth, who was born in the year 1951, to find a niche in the history of Indo-English writing in India. *A Suitable Boy* has the body of Indian theme and clothes of Western novel. All important characters assemble at the wedding of Lata.

NOTES

1. Vikram Seth in an interview to Seema Paul, *The Telegraph Magazine*, 21 February 1993, p. 9.
2. Viney Kirpal, *The Journal of Commonwealth Literature*, Vol. XXVI, No. 1, 1991, p. 150.
3. Vikram Seth in an interview to Seema Paul, p. 9.

Yinglish in *A Suitable Boy*

S. Gopal, commenting on Indian English writes: "India is not a country with a large community of British settlers who might have resisted the influence of the local context. Nor is English in India, as in the Caribbean, the sole means of communication. The languages of India have a history which in most cases go back over 1,000 years; and just as English has influenced them during the last 100 years, they now influence English. They give it an indigenous flavour and promote a new idiom." To understand the nuances of Indian culture, in any foreign language, one has to fall for words Indian to grasp its real contour. Rudyard Kipling and E.M. Forster, in *Kim* and *A Passage to India* respectively, heighten the pitch of one's immediate consciousness of one's surrounding. James Joyce had extended the range of English, deliberately, to convey the Irishness in his novels. To be a successful writer, one has to breathe in the native air, draw sustenance from the native vocabulary, idioms, phrases, customs, myths and religious rites.

The starting point of Indo-English writing began with poets like Henry Louis Vivian Derozio, Michael Madhusudan Dutta, Sarojini Naidu, Sri Aurobindo Ghosh, or novelists like R.C. Dutta, S.K. Ghosh, A. Madhaviah and T. Ramakrishna Pillai. These creative writings, ab initio, produced, amongst writers and readers, a sense of confidence, exuberance, exhilaration and elan—that they can use a foreign language, creatively.

The second turning point in the growth and expansion of Indo-English creative writing came with the rise of Gandhi on the Indian horizon. This period can be termed as the teenage period in Indo-English literature. Lots of beards and moustaches were growing on the chins, there was that impetuous and unhindered rush, which, on the crest of freedom movement, under Gandhi, found expression in politics, political jargon and vocabulary, myths, stories and folklores. Gandhi, though himself not a prolific writer in English, seasoned the exuberance with his basic simple English using "homely analogy (e.g. his description of the charkha as 'not a new invention [but] a re-discovery; a happy knack of coining memorable phrases like 'Himalayan blunder,' 'Satanic Government,' 'poem of pity' (description of the cow) and 'Drain Inspector's Report' (apropos of Miss Mayo's attack on India)."[2] Pandit Nehru and Dr. Radhakrishnan wrote impeccable English. Among the novelists, K.S. Venkataramani, A.S.P. Ayyar, K. Narayan, Mulk Raj Anand, R.K. Narayan and Raja Rao, it is Anand whose "style, at its best, is redolent of the Indian soil, as a result of his bold importation into English of words, phrases, expletives, turns of expression and proverbs drawn from his native Punjabi and Hindi."[3] Most of the novelists of his generation never got opportunities to study at Oxford, Cambridge or some other universities of the U.K. That led R.K. Narayan to write: "We are not attempting to write Anglo-Saxon English. The English language, through sheer resilience and mobility, is now undergoing a process of Indianization in the same manner as it adopted U.S. citizenship over a hundred years ago, with the difference that it is the major language there but here one of the fifteen. . . . All that I am able to confirm, after nearly thirty years of writing [written in 1964] is that it has served my purpose admirably, of conveying unambiguously the thoughts and acts of a set of personalities, who flourish in a small town named Malgudi (supposed to be) located in a corner of South India."[4] Anand counted 900 Indian words in the Oxford English Dictionary, in 1972. Since then, many more have been added to the O.E.D., Anand himself has added more than fifty words. Raja Rao describes the process of Indians writing in English, in the following words:

> One has to convey in a language, that is not one's own the spirit that is one's own. One has to convey the various shades and omissions of a certain thought movement that look maltreated in an alien language. I used the word alien. Yet English is not really an alien language to us. We are all instinctively bilingual, many of us writing in our own language and in English. We cannot write like the English. We should

not. We can write only as Indians. We have grown to look at the large world as part of us.

The independence of India in 1947, the partition of the country into two, and communal riots following the partition provided fodder to some talented and intelligent writers to churn out some outstanding novels, notably, *So Many Hungers* by Bhabani Bhattacharya, *Train to Pakistan* by Khushwant Singh, *The Dark Dancer* by B. Rajan, *A Bend in the Ganges* by Manohar Malgonkar, *And Gazelles Leaping* by Sudhindra Nath Ghosh and *All about H. Hatterr* by G.V. Desani, to name only a few. This post-Gandhi, beginning from 1947 till the eighties, can be called the years of the adulthood of novels written in English by Indians. Adapting the craft of using Indians words, expressions and sensibilities, initiated by Mulk Raj Anand, Bhabani Bhattacharya, Khushwant Singh, Manohar Malgonkar and G.V. Desani accelerated and directed it more vigorously and honestly. Bhattacharya's use of Indianisms is judicious whereas Singh's is overdone, like that of Anand. "Malgonkar's use of mutilated Anglicized forms of names like 'Tantya' (for 'Tatya') and 'Dhondu Pant' (for 'Dhondo Pant') can be explained by his pucka sahib proclivities."[5]

The eighties are the greening period of Indian fiction writing in English. The award of the Booker Prize to Salman Rushdie, in 1981, for his metafiction *Midnight's Children* kindled fresh hopes in the skeptics who predicted the pre-mature death of Indo-English fiction. His third novel, *Shame,* skyrocketed his credentials as a major novelist, of international standard. His success boosted the sagging morale of the talented writers in India and some big names, like Amitav Ghosh, Upamanyu Chatterjee, Shashi Deshpande, Nina Sibal, Pratap Sharma and Vikram Seth emerged out of the shadows of the past and found responses from Indian and foreign publishers, readers and critics.

The interlarding of the vernacular with English or vice-versa, initiated by Anand, journeyed into books of several novelists, in a stereotyped style, often, unnatural and stale. "It was Salman Rushdie, however, who in his *Midnight's Children* successfully exploited the creative potential of the quaint English spoken in the bazaars and homes in India and, in the words of Anita Desai, 'Set free the tongues of those young Indian writers who wished to express the contemporary spirit but had not found an authentic and relevant way to do so."[6] Vikram Seth, like Salman Rushdie, exploited the creative potential of English in *A Suitable Boy*, his range is greater and his locale is different and his texture is denser.

If the localism of Rushdie is Indian bazaar, that of Seth is the Chatterjees, the Mehras, the Kapoors, the Nawabs, all belonging to either highly anglicized society or upper and lower middle class society of the early fifties, when the use of Indian English was yet to enchant the Indian bazaar or overpower the common people. Therefore, the Indianisms of *A Suitable Boy* are confined to the upper or lower middle class society and that helps Seth to delineate characters, their social mores and their mind-sets in varieties of Indian English—Hinglish, Bengalish, Tanglish, Urglish and Pucka Sahibish. Though I don't pose myself as a Sherlock Holmes, or a forensic expert, I have been able to comb nearly 118 Indian words, Indian expressions and Pucka Sahibish words. As mentioned above, they have been broadly put into four categories viz. 66 Hinglish (or Punjabi) words, 14 Banglish words, 20 Urglish words, 15 Pucka Sahibish words and 3 Tanglish words, all written in their native expressions and dialects.

First, I shall examine the use of Hinglish words and expressions in *A Suitable Boy*. While examining them, I shall refer to Anand and Singh, the predecessors of Seth, and find out how effective the amalgamation of Hinglish into Standard English is? Take, for instance, the following lines: "Exams are coming up, Malatiji, and you are still buying novels? Twelves annas plus one rupee four annas makes two rupees altogether. I should not allow this. You are like daughter to me." (47) No Englishman will ever say "Exams are coming up," for "come up" means "come to a place or position regarded as higher." (C.O.D) He would say: "Exams are approaching." The mention of annas gives local colour, the period of 1951, when the use of decimal coins did not come into vogue in India. Besides, no realist would expect a provincial book-seller to speak impeccable English, in 1951.

A conservative wife, in North India, does not call her husband by name. A typical village woman, in Anand, refers to her husband as "they" and does not mention his name. The novelist informs the reader: "And Sajnu had walked by the house with 'them.' . . . And she had stolen a look and nearly met 'their' eyes." (*The Road*, 5) Similarly, Mrs. Mahesh Kapoor, "when referring to her husband, often called him 'Minister Sahib.' Sometimes, in Hindi she even called him 'Pran's father.' To refer to him by name would have been unthinkable, Even 'my husband' was unacceptable to her, but 'my this' was all right." (177) Even Mrs. Rupa Mehra, a widow, calls her husband not by name but by using 'He,' or 'Him.' On the other hand, the anglicized Meenakshi, the daughter-in-law of Mrs. Mehra, does not hesitate to call her husband Arun by name. This regionalism adds beauty as well as timeless values of the North Indian societies.

Like Raja Rao and Mulk Raj Anand, Seth uses the device of "translation" of words and expressions. Raja Rao writes: "You cannot straighten a dog's tail." Mulk Raj Anand writes: "'My son,' said Gujri with an affectionate pout, pouring another glass of whey. 'Look, he has come in the heat. And he must be hungry and thirsty. May I be his sacrifice!'" Vikram Seth writes:

> After she had returned it, the Ustad sang a few phrases of a slow alap for her to imitate, but her performance was so unsatisfactory that at one point he said sharply to her: "Listen, Listen first, Listen first, then sing. Listening is fifteen annas in the rupee. Reproducing it is one anna—it's the work of a parrot." (294)

Vikram Seth, very graphically and meticulously describes the preparation of Khaini, in the following words: "He was rolling some tobacco in his palm with the thumb of his other hand. He rubbed it, then tamped it down, threw off the excess, examined the residue with care, selected out the impurities, took a pinch, licked the inside of his lower lip, and spat out a bit sideways onto the floor." (501) This is one of the many examples of Indo-English writers's deliberate design to put across the peculiarities of Indian customs and manners to the foreign reader. The hero of B. Rajan's *The Dark Dancer* explains the ways and stages of making idli and sambhar, two South Indian culinary specialities. Raja Rao in his "Notes" to *Kanthapura* describes dhoti as "a fabric used for loinclothes by Indian men; also the loin-cloth itself. The manner of tying a dhoti is a subject of considerable attention, and may vary from a simple three-cornered diaper to a complex pajama."

Khushwant Singh specialized in faithfully depicting the vernacular of Punjabi villagers. The Punjabi dialect abounds in the use of four-letter words. In *Train to Pakistan,* the village Lambardar expressed his anguish and anger to Meet Singh on the insult meted out to Imam Baksh by the Sikh army officer. He said: "And didn't you see how that pig's penis spoke to Chacha." (39) Anand writes in *The Road* "Maro Sale Ko! Kill him!" (110) In *A Suitable Boy* Waris, out of anger, abuses the Munshi of the Nawab: "No, No, Maan Sahib, why bother? A hornet bites the haramzada's penis at four-forty every day." (640) Again, Seth makes the Pathan speak to his co-passengers: "Bastards! I, one man alone, beat up three of them, and no one raised a hand to help me. I'm saving your money and your wealth for you." (527) The Raja of Marh goes to the Kumbha Mela: "'Hurry up, hurry up!' shouted the Raja, as he stumbled down the long ramp to the sands. 'Where is this Sanaki Baba's camp? Where do all these sister-fucking pilgrims come from? Isn't there any organization? Get me my car!'" (705)

Singh's character Jugga apprehends Malli returning from the village and refers to him as "that incestuous lover of his sister." (*Train to Pakistan,* 15) As mentioned earlier, Salman Rushdie also picks up Indian bazaar language to weave it into Standard English to heighten the local colour and idiom of the place, and now Tai Bai leaning out of a window shouts, "Hey, bhaenchud! little sister-sleeper, where you running? What's true is true is true?" (*Midnight's Children*, 320)

Vikram Seth uses political slogans, repeatedly heard, either before a leader starts speechifying or in the middle of his speech or at the end of his speech, in northern India:

(1) "Baitar Ka MLA Kaisa ho?" cried someone from the podium.
 "Ramlal Sinha Jaisa ho!" shouted the crowd. (1173)
(2) "Zindabad!"

"Jawaharlal Nehru—"
"Zindabad!"
"Minister Mahesh Kapoor Sahib—"
"Zindabad!"
"Congress Party—"
"Jai—"
"Hindi!" (1176)

(3) Seth translates the first slogan into English:
"The MLA from Baitar, how should he be?"
His supporters in the crowd shouted back in rhyme:
"Ramlal, one such as he!" (1171)

Political slogans of the type mentioned above, are common refrains, only in northern India and any attempt to translate (1) into (3) fails because it cannot catch the tone and nuance of Hinglish, so necessary to make a work of art seem natural.

Vikram Seth often makes efforts at transcreation and not merely translation. We shall take only two examples, out of many.

(1) Better than all the world is this our Hindustan.
    We are its nightingales, it is our rose garden.   (1172)
(2) Don't break the thread of love, Raheem has said.
    What breaks won't join; if joined, it knots the thread. (1135)

Achebe uses popular songs to create mood and atmosphere, as well as to offer perspective on the character's action and viewpoint. The first song mentioned above shows the mood of patriotism and the action of creating an atmosphere of favourable political climate for his election. The second song is indicative of the pensive mood of Jagat Ram. If Seth were Anand or Singh, he would, instead of transcreating the lines, have written in Hindi. That would have helped his Hindi readers to understand the lines better. But, writing in 1993, Seth, unlike Anand and Singh, is in a stronger position to cover the whole spectrum of Indian society—North, South, East and West. R.K. Narayan, in spite of his Standard English, remained South Indian writer and M.R. Anand, for his Hinglish, remained a North Indian novelist. Seth excels both of them in painting on a larger canvas, including Indians of all tongues.

Describing the Chatterjees, Seth, in a linguistic feat, uses Banglish, successfully. Bengali prose-style reached a fixed elegant literary standard in the writings of Bankim Chandra Chatterjee. Before him there were currents and cross-currents, some following the highly Sanskritised verbosity, some leaning towards a Persianised vocabulary, some preferring the colloquial—others often taking to a graceless hotch-potch. Bengali language and pronunciation in English is uniquely Bengali, unlike the Punjabi living in and around Delhi. For instance, for 'gazal,' a Bengali utters 'gojol.' (291) The *'bhadralok of Calcutta,'* (384) according to Nirad C. Chaudhuri are "gentlefolk or, as we say in Bengali, *Bhadra Lok*—a class based equally on occupation and on birth, [in them] there is complete elasticity in spite of the infinite gradations of wealth and standard of living which are to be found within the order and which often range from extreme poverty to extreme luxury."[7] It is the middle-class within the middle-class, without which the influential and stable Bengali *bhadralok* could not have maintained the health, hold, and power of their order. The womenfolk never resist gaudy trifles. In *A Suitable Boy*, Kakoli and Meenakshi endlessly rhyme and mime. "'But half the *bhadralok* in Calcutta want him as a match for their daughter,' added Meenakshi. 'They believe he [Amit] has brains.'" Kakoli recited:

> Amit Chatterjee, what a catch!
> Is a highly suitable match!

Meenakshi added:

> Why he has not married yet?
> Always playing hard to get.

Kakoli continued:

> Famous poet, so they say.
> "Besh" decent in every way. (384-85)

Seth, very subtly, introduces the Chatterjees, calling them

bhadralok and, then, in doggerels, describes the gaudy trifles of their womenfolk and later on, their menfolk also. 'Besh' is a Bengali word meaning 'alright.'

These *bhadralok*, in general, were contemptuous of everything provincial and they suffered from cultural superiority, partly because of English education and richness and identity of their own culture and, partly because of their metropolitan chauvinism. That's why Dr. Ila Choudhary says to Lata about Brahmpur: "It made me almost ill. All that courtly culture with its Yes Hazoor and No Huzoor and nothing robust about it at all. 'How are you?' 'Oh, well, I'm alive.' . . . All that subtlety and etiquette and bowing and scraping and ghazals and Kathak." (393)

Besides the world of the *bhadraloks* there is also a world of "Biswas Baby's adda." (475) People belonging to lower middle class, having no drawing rooms in their houses and no other source of entertainments, like that of the Chatterjees, met at a fixed place. Nirad C. Chaudhuri vividly described one such *adda*: "Every able-bodied person after his return from office and a hurried wash and tea rushed out of his house with the intention of meeting his friends. . . . The more usual practice, however, was to avoid these misadventures by having fixed rendezvous or, as they were called in Bengali, *adda*. Each *adda* had its fixed adherents, who would begin to drop in one by one from about half-past five in the afternoon till in about an hour's time the attendance was full. These gathering-places were most often the outer parlor of one of the wealthier members of the group, but at times also an office after office hours, and, more rarely, a tea-shop."[8] In *A Suitable Boy*, we find a description of one such adda: "Biswas Babu's adda or den had slowly cemented this (Biswas Babu's with the *burra babu* of the insurance department of Bentsen Pryce) relationship. . . . The *burra babu* would visit Biswas Babu's house most evenings; here a number of old companions would gather to talk about the world or simply to sit around, drinking tea and reading the newspapers with an occasional comment." (475)

These two worlds in *A Suitable Boy* clearly and sharply differentiate the likes of Chatterjees or Biswas babus, their social mores and family lives, their intellectual gains, their modes of entertainments and so on and so forth. Not only that, Vikram

Seth has successfully delineated Bengali culture—one of the earliest and most important limbs of Indian culture. Then, he uses some Bengali words to add flavour to the narrative. We quote some examples below:

(1) "Truly—but you must try the luchis." (400) "Luchis" in Hindi is "puris."
(2) "Mr. Justice Chatterji, who was wearing a *dhoti-kurta*." (418) It is a part of Bengali culture for menfolk to wear *dhoti-kurta* either when they are relaxing or on holidays or on the days of pujas.
(3) "*Ki Korcho tumi*, Dipankar ?" (477)
(4) "*And mishti doi.*" (461)
(5) "His wife was fat, highly emotional woman who wore a great deal of sindoor in her hair.... She was a shocking gossip and in between extracting fine fishbones from her large paan-stained mouth." (461)

One could see women chewing paan in almost all middle-class families in Bengal.

Nirad C. Chaudhuri, writing on the anglicized *bhadralok*, comments: "The old type could always be distinguished from the normal run of Bengalis, and were invariably called Sahibs instead of Babus. Their wives too were addressed as Memsahibs."[9] Biswas Babu is called Babu for he belongs to the general run of Bengalis but the Chatterjees are invariably called Sahibs. Bahadur addresses Tapan as "Baby Sahib," (403) Mrs Chatterjee as "Memsahib." (403)

The use of Tanglish is associated with Professor Jaikumar. Professor Jaikumar is a South Indian Professor of English and is shown, in the novel, to be on the board of interview to select a reader in the Department of English, Brahmpur University. He says: "'Our typical young university teacher,' he began, 'is overworked when he is junior—he has to teach yelementary prose and compulsory Yinglish. If he is yinnately conscientious, he has no time for yennything else. By then the fire is out—.'" (1272) He continues his conversation further: "And also we may know too much by then and have no yexpress motivation for writing. Writing is yitself discovery. Yexplication in yexploration!" (1273) Any foreigner or even Indian would be appalled at his choice of words beginning with dangerous vowels but this is the exact use of the nationalized English. Devindra Kohli explains this: "And listening to the Welsh variation, or to the Yorkshire English in which 'come' becomes 'coom' and 'up' becomes 'oop,' I was reminded of the rather endearing way in which a South Indian makes some of his 'o' into 'e' and prefixes 'y' and 'w,' respectively, in words beginning with 'e' or 'o.'"[10] In Professor Jaikumar, Vikram Seth gives the distinct flavour of South Indian English and, thus, gives us a glimpse of South Indian culture.

The expansion of Muslims in India in early medieval times is an event of vast lingual significance. Mutual intercourse between the newcomers and the Indian people, and the many new things which the Muslims had brought about them, necessitated the use of a mixed vocabulary which could be understood by both. Thus, a new language was born, Urdu. It incorporated many words from Persian and through the Persian many words from Arabic and Turkish came in. Then, it absorbed many words from Brij, Khadi Boli and Haryanvi. In *A Suitable Boy*, Urdu is spoken by the Nawab, members of his family and his minions, on the one hand, and the courtesan, Saeeda Bai and his followers, on the other. First of all, we take up the Nawab and his family. Like the Chatterjees, steeped in the English culture with Sahibs and Memsahibs, the Nawabs are steeped in the old aristocratic northern Indian Muslim culture. In place of Sahibs and Memsahibs in English, we, here, hear "Chhote Sahib," (102) "the Nawab Sahib," (271) "Huzoor" etc. The vocabulary concerning family is as usual, in Urdu style. We compare some Urdu words with Bengali and Hindi.

(i) "Ammi-Jaan" (321) with "Ma" (377) in Hindi and "Mago" (395) in Bengali.
(ii) "Abba-Jaan" (271) with "Baba (419) in Bengali and "Baoji" (6) in Hindustani.
(iii) "Abida Chachi" (277) with "Ila Kaki" (462) in Bengali.

Another distinctive feature of Muslim culture, shown in *A Suit-*

able Boy, is the culture of marriage. Maan is more than twenty-three when he meets Rasheed's father. He says: "Not being married is considered by my religion and yours to be . . . *Adharma*." (668) He continues to say: "Our religion says that the *izzat*, the honour of an unmarried is half that of a married man." (669) Then, talking about his Baba and his three marriages, he says: "*Marte gae, Karte gae*. When one died he married another." (699) The figurative and sensuous imagery brings Seth's readers closer to his narrative.

Keeping a dancing girl as one's mistress by the Muslim aristocrats is a common refrain in almost all Urdu literary and social scenes. In *Twilight in Delhi*, Mir Nihar, an aristocrat, keeps a mistress Babban Jan, a young and beautiful dancing girl. His son, Asghar, too has a sweet-heart, Mushtari Bai, a graceful dancing girl. In *A Suitable Boy*, the Nawab Sahib, in his young age, had a mistress and Tasneem is their daughter. His son, Firoz, also frequents the house of Saeeda Bai in the foot-steps of his father. To communicate the total and intensified picture of the Muslim ethos, Vikram Seth has given vivid and brief description of the various Muslim customs, social and religious ceremonies and festivals, in Urglish and Urdu. Examples are given below:

(1) "The tall, grey-bearded Nawab Sahib . . . gravely raised his cupped hand to his forehead in polite salutation." (18) It is an unique Muslim social custom of salutation.
(2) "Hashim, almost in tears, did *adaab* to Saeeda Bai, and walked out of the courtyard." (86)

One more example of salutation has sinister nuance and raises human temper and tastes its credulity. According to Muslim politician-scholar Dr. Rafiq Zakaria, "In the Quoran the word 'Kafir' is applied to those who conceal or deny ('Kufr') the existence of God (and thus '*Kafir* or non-believers') are those who make others partners with God or sharers with God, thus 'Mushrik,' those who deny the oneness of God."[11]

Saeeda Bai's ghazals form part of Urglish in *A Suitable Boy*. "Saeeda Bai enjoyed most of all singing from the ghazals of Mir and Ghalib." (82) Mir's subjective poetry symbolizes the tragedy of common man, toiling under feudal fatalism, Saeeda Bai sings a couplet, of this theme, in the house of Mahesh Kapoor on the occasion of the marriage of his son Pran Kapoor to Savita Mehra: "We who were helpless were accused of independent thought and deed. They did whatever they desired, and us they smeared with calumny." (87) She also sings from the ghazals of Ghalib, "Where have those meetings and those partings gone?" And, finally, sings a few favourite lines from a minor poet, Minai:

> The meeting has dispersed; the moths
> Bid farewell to the candle-light.
> Departure's hour is on the sky.
> Only a few stars mark the night.

This way, Urglish of Vikram Seth comes to help the readers know their India and its multifaceted culture, language and dialect.

We also try to fish out some words and expressions, reminiscent of Britishers, especially rulers, using for their subordinates. Arun Mehta and his wife Meenakshi are the vestiges of this class.

(3) "For many years now, the Nawab Sahib had visited his wife's grave as often as possible to read the *fatiha* over it." (320) It is, once again, an unique Muslim religious rite.

(4) "Rasheed explained to Maan a little later where they could have to go for their morning toilet—out in the fields with a brass *lota* to carry water in." (509)

Religious ceremonies are also mentioned in *A Suitable Boy*, in Urglish. I give three examples from the text:

(i) "Well?" said Baba. "Get up, get up. As it says in the call, prayer is better than sleep."

"Actually,"—Maan found his voice at last—"I don't go to prayer."

"You don't read the *namaaz*?" Baba looked more than injured. (509)

(2) "That's the local school, the *madrasa*," said Rasheed matter-of-factly. . . . "No—well, yes, some of course. . . . He liked

Brahmpur because life was less narrow and frustrating there than in the rigid and—in his view—reactionary village." (511)

(3) "Everything is scientific for you," said Qamar. "Even the caste system. Even worshipping the linga and other disgusting things. And singing bhajans to that adulterer, that teaser of women, that thief Krishna."

Then, there is the use of '*Kafir*' for Hindus by Muslims.

Finally, we find the literal translation of Hindi and Urdu expressions into English to get, once again, a local colour:

(1) "How long will you be conferring on us the honour of your presence?" (1008)
(2) "Electricity does not grow on trees." (1131)
(3) "Now what may Huzoor's poor munshi fetch him?" (636)
(4) "No use, except to eat money." (524)
(5) "We come empty-handed into this world and go out empty-handed. Do you have to lie so early in the morning? Will you take this money with you when you go?" (164)
(6) "Come in, come in, Dagh Sahib. Sit down and illumine our gathering." (1099)

The Coleridgean definition of good prose as "proper words in their proper place" is particularly significant in relation to the order of words and patterns of sentences commonly used by Indian creative writers in English. Indian writers, like Vikram Seth, frequently break all rules of grammar to do creative writing in the Indian-English. Their path-finders, in different times, are three Irish writers, George Moore, George Bernard Shaw and James Joyce who took liberty with the strict rules of Nesfield, coined new words and enriched the English language with vivacious prose. James Stephens reported, on meeting Joyce, "He . . . confided the secret to me . . . that, grammatically, I did not know the difference between a semi-colon and a colon . . . and that I should give up writing."[12] In Samuel Beckett's *Fizzles* the Irish word *desil* (which means clockwise) suddenly appears, and we recall that it is also used conspicuously as the first word in the Oxen of the Sun episode in *Ulysses*. The Irishness of Joyce's books was a distinguishing mark. But the tragedy with Indian writers is that they, like Professor Higgins of Shaw's *Pygmalion*, take up pidgin English like Eliza Doolittle, teach her Standard English and pass her off as a Duchess of India, i.e. pigeon English and, then, drop her off on to the mercy of the 'weak and poor' Fueddy Hill. The emotional and intellectual integration of pigeon English into Standard English, like that of Irish English into Queen's or King's English, of Shaw and Joyce, fails to arouse that Indian ardour, flavour, nuance and intensity that Shaw and Joyce depicted successfully. I have written earlier that Salman Rushdie harnessed the creativeness of pigeon English in his novels and so does Seth in *A Suitable Boy*.

NOTES

1. Sarvepalli Gopal, *Encounter*, July/August 1989, Vol. LXXII, No. 2, p. 18.
2. M.K. Naik, *A History of Indian English Literature* (New Delhi: Sahitya Akademi, 1992), p. 125.
3. *Ibid.*, p. 160.
4. R.K. Narayan, "English in India: The Process of Transmutation," *Aspects of Indian Writing in English* (Macmillan India, 1979), p. 22.
5. M.K. Naik, p. 219.
6. Devindra Kohli, "A Tragic Love Affair? The Contemporary Indian-English Literary Scene," *Aspects of Commonwealth Literature*, Vol. I (Oct. 1988-June 1989).
7. Nirad C. Chaudhuri, *The Autobiography of an Unknown Indian* (Bombay: Jaico, 1969), p. 383.
8. *Ibid.*, p. 398.
9. *Ibid.*, p. 403.
10. Devindra Kohli, pp. 3-4.
11. Rafiq Zakaria, "Gandhi, Islam and Secularism" in *Gandhi and Communal Harmony* (New Delhi: Gandhi Smriti and Darshan Samiti, 1991), p. 1.
12. Quoted in Richard Ellman's *James Joyce* (New York: Oxford University Press, 1959), p. 345.

The Tajmahal and the Victoria Memorial: The Novels of Salman Rushdie and Vikram Seth

Of all the Indo-English novelists, writing since the thirties, only Salman Rushdie and Vikram Seth have metamorphosed the provincial, tradition-bound and sheepish novel into one of the most important, innovative, open and dew-fresh forms of writing, rivalling novels of international standard. These two princes charming by their literary callisthenics turned the mulatto-novel into a new shape, a form, an identity, a recognition so far denied to it in the international literature fora, since its re-birth in India. What is more, they kindled fresh hopes into ember of the growing body of novelists, born after 1947, unaffected by the horrors and tortures of the partition, untouched by the fiery idealism of Gandhi. Pt. Nehru and Mrs. Gandhi, their socialist and secular policies and their failure to live up to great expectations haunt the writings of the new generation, writing in the eighties. The eighties, in fact, are the greening period in the history of the Indo-English novel writing.

Rushdie, the torch-bearer and path-finder, was, like George Eliot, Henry James, James Joyce (in novel) and T.S. Eliot (in poetry), an intellectual novelist, who unlike his predecessors, handcuffed history to fiction and fiction to fantasy, autobiography, time and writing. His *Midnight's Children* and *Shame* show his omniscient point of view. In the former, Rushdie and Saleem and in the latter Rushdie through Omar Khayyam, mix up their personal and national histories of India and Pakistan and, then weave them into fantasy and suspense to create some sort of "trailers" of an episodic cinema. A close analysis of *Midnight's Children* would reveal the structure of an episodic film or serial with that of the metafiction—chapter by chapter progression of the metafiction, like an episodic film, provides a rhythmical counterpoint to the tantalizing teasers which anticipates events to come. Rushdie also employs sensationalism of thrillers to hold the attention of his literati. Narrative synopses "provide Saleem with a means of compensating for this sensationalism by imposing order and significance on past events."

Vikram Seth also handcuffs history to *A Suitable Boy* not with the aids of fantasy and autobiography but with the aids of time and writing. *Midnight's Children* shows Saleem's family trials and tribulations linked with Indian history—the various births, labours and deaths correspond exactly to major events in Indian history: the Jallianwallah Bagh massacre, Nehru's 'tryst with destiny,' Indira Gandhi's rise to and tenacious hold on power, her Emergency rule, her trial. A very long period indeed. Seth's fiction is posited in a very specific period, 1951-52, the period of intense political in-fightings in the Congress Party, between the Tandonites and the Nehruites, the communal disharmony, the cultural slavery of the anglicized Indians and the search for an 'ism' for Indian political, social and economic policies. Seth, unlike Rushdie, does not intrude into the terrains of his metafiction with omniscient point of view. The goal of Seth is very modest—the telescoping of the period, 1951-52, in 1349 pages. Then, he hovers about, interposes between characters (real and invented) and incidents and invigilates, whenever necessary. The minute and concentrated treatment of a small period makes the study and reading of *A Suitable Boy* more intense, appealing and comprehensible. On the other hand, the goal of Rushdie is wider and his telescoping of the Indian history—thirty years of colonial and thirty years of free India—in 558 pages, makes the treatment of this period, in the metafiction, sweeping, difficult and at times, mind-bending. By writing this, I do not propose to minimize the literary callisthenics of Rushdie in the face of Seth's feeble entry into the gymnasium, itself.

Rushdie is undoubtedly among the immortals of the art of parody. *Midnight's Children*, the mock-epic of post-independence India, is punctuated with parodies of many scandals that shook the nation. The Nanavati case of seduction and murder cutting short one of the most promising naval officer careers of the country is parodied in the story of the narrator's Buckingham Villa (which is itself a parody of Buckingham Palace, echoing the seat of British royalty), neighbour Homi Catrack, the seducer of his other neighbour, Lila Sabarmati, being shot by the injured husband Commander Sabarmati. Seth employs burlesque in place of parody, realism of presentation in place of verism, comedy in place of fantasy and history in place of history-autobiography. No scandal of the Nanavati nature and immenseness is discussed in *A Suitable Boy*. Only small and local scandals—that of the Nawab with a courtesan and Maan's with Saeeda Bai or Sahgal's ineffectual advance towards his niece Lata—form a small part of the novel. The scandals surrounding Kidwai and Agarwal are confined to the party level, are not 'fatal fliers.' Meenakshi's illicit relation with Billy Irani does not break into national scandal like that of Lila Sabarmati with Homi Catrack.

Rushdie is well-versed in English literature and he uses this knowledge via parody with devastating effect, unique in the history of the Indo-English novel writing. As samples, I quote two examples: (1) "No: I'm no monster, nor have I been guilty of trickery. I provided clues" (*MC*, 118) echoes "The Love Song of J. Alfred Prufrock" of T.S. Eliot:

> No: I am not Prince Hamlet, nor was meant to be:
> Am an attendant lord, one that will do
> To swell a progress, start a scene or two,
> Advise the prince; no doubt, an easy tool,
> Deferential, glad to be of use....   111-15)

(2) The introductory passage of Chapter VII of *Shame:* "Between shame and shamelessness lies the axis upon which we turn," (115) echoes lines in Eliot's "The Hollow Men":

> Between the emotion
> And the response
> Passes the shadow ...
> Between the ascent
> And the descent
> Falls the shadow ...

This marriage of parody with literary allusions has been aptly termed literary callisthenics. Seth, in *A Suitable Boy,* employs literary allusions from English literature, Indian epics, *Koran,* Tagore and Urdu poets. He uses these collages to serve as burlesque, to create wider horizons, to intensify the character-delineation and to give an effect of suspense.

(1) Better than all the world is this our Hindustan
    We are its nightingale, it is our rose-garden.   (1172)

It was written by Iqbal who, flushed with religious harmony and the unity of India, composed this poem, only to retract afterwards. He, instead, became the great exponent of the division of India along religious line and he was not 'its nightingale.' But Ramlal Sinha uses the poem to arouse patriotism among his listeners, during the Assembly election in 1952:

(2) Dipankar recites Tagore's poetry on rural Bengal.
    I bow, I bow to my beautiful motherland Bengal:
    To your river-banks, to your winds that cool and console; ...
    Your shrouded villages, that are nests of shade and peace.
                                                           (1103-4)

Seth's remark is self-explanatory, "Not that Calcutta contained any of the above-mentioned features." Both the examples show the hollow men and women in *A Suitable Boy*—Ramlal Sinha, Mrs. Chatterjee, Dipankar and Tapan.

Themes of *Midnight's Children* and *Shame* are centred on squandered talents, failed dreams and ideologies and idealism gone berserk. Verism is the key-word for them. Saleem, at his birth in 1947, symbolizes the exuberance and promise of an emergent nation. In the fifties, his exuberance slowly gives way to disillusionment, "All over India I stumble across good Indian businessmen, their fortune-thriving, thanks to the first five years plans." (*MC,* 176) Another point of tension is between idealism and violence. Midnight's Children Conference is the reflection of this tension, Saleem and Shiva being two opposing protagonists. The former representss idealism and the latter violence and practicality. All the ugly pimples of India's face, namely, linguistic, religious, caste, class and provincial re-surface. Finally, the imposition of the Emergency, in 1975, doomed the children of hope of 1947 into violent destruction. *Shame* is about Pakistan-Islamic fundamentalism, repressive society, careerism, "cops, politics, revenge, assassinations, executions, blood and guts."[1] Shame is a part of "the architecture of the society that the novel dsecribes."

Themes of *A Suitable Boy* are about the search of India for its social, cultural, educational and political milieu interwoven with Mrs. Rupa Mehra and Lata, the Chatterjees, Prof. Mishra and Pran, L.N. Agarwal and Mahesh Kapoor and their searches. The political figures—Tandon, Nehru, Kidwai, J.P. and Lohia—course through the veins of the invented characters in *A Suitable Boy*, effortlessly and hopefully. In Rushdie, a political figure like General Zia is Raza Hyder (*Shame*) or General Ayub is 'Commander of pepperpots' (*MC*, 315) and the literary device of roman-a-clef, employed thoroughly in Rushdie, is not used in Seth. Still, some similarities exist between Rushdie and Seth. The Narlikar women (*MC*) are also the traders of Misri Mandi (*ASB*), Shiva (*MC*) is Waris, Agarwal and king of Marh rolled into one and Saleem (*MC*) is Mahesh Kapoor. (*ASB*) Seth's use of pastiche, like Eliot, from English literature, Hindu prayers, Christians' Lord's Prayer and other sources fit neatly into the context and they help to parody the characters. *A Suitable Boy*, on the other hand, may be called the epigone of Eliot's poetry and Rushdie's novels. Rushdie with the "poet's eye, in a fine frenzy rolling/Doth glance from heaven to Earth, from earth to heaven." Seth, like a stream flows stilly, occasionally drying up, nonetheless chortling. Rushdie is the novelist for the literati; Seth is for literati and l'homme moyen sensuel, both.

Rushdie patterns *Midnight's Children* after the episodic and digressive mode of the *Ramayana* i.e., the circular narrative technique of some of his predecessors, like Narayan, Anand and Raja Rao. What Saleem attempts by writing the novel is to follow the Indian urge to "encapsulate the whole of reality." (75) With some irritation, he remarks that "no people whose word for 'yesterday' is the same as their word for 'tomorrow' can be said to have a firm grip on the time," (106) and the narrator in *Shame* also pinpoints this as the central problem in his attempt to narrate the story of Khayyam, remarking that "it seems that the future cannot be restrained, and insists on seeping back on the past." (24) What Vikram Seth does is to follow a chronological view of Indian history, imposed on the Indian national consciousness by the British and this needs the linear narrative, the act of plotting, to describe its cause-and-effect basis. The political in-fightings between the Tandonites and the Nehruites, the assumption of the Congress Presidency by Nehru, the assassination of Pakistan's Prime Minister, Liaquat Ali Khan, the Abolition of the Zamindari and the election of Parliament and the State Assembly, all zero in on 1951-52, chronologically. Seth writes, "1952: the fresh and brilliant digits impressed themselves upon Pran's eye as he opened the morning newspaper." (1138) Seth has said so in an interview, "Well, this novel is linear partly because it's multilinear."[2]

The importation of Indian language into *Midnight's Children*, *Shame* and *A Suitable Boy* is a 'chutnification' of English language. In the first two books, chutney consists of three ingredients, viz. Standard English, Hindi and Urdu and in the last book, it consists of six—standard English, Hinglish, Urglish, Tanglish, Bangalish and Pucka Sahibish. At the hands of Anand and Singh the chutney, by daily use, became stale and tasteless. It "was Salman Rushdie, however, who in his *Midnight's Children* successfully exploited the creative potential of the quaint English spoken in the bazaars and homes in India and, in the words of Anita Desai, "set free the tongues of those young Indian writers who wished to express the contemporary spirit but had not found an authentic and relevant way to do so."[3] Seth is a follower of Rushdie but his range is greater. First of all, Rushdie and Seth use the literary method of reduplication in flawless English for fluent effect.

(1) "'*Chhi, chhi,*" Padma covers her ears, "My God, such a *dirty-filthy* man, I never knew!" (*MC,* 319)

(2) "These badmashes would not get away with their *whistling shistling* if it was my affair!" (*S,* 61)

(3) "*Kissing, missing,* every day,
    Cuddling, muddling all the way." (*ASB,* 881)

(4) "What do you think people will think of all that *ghich-pich* when they receive it." (*ASB,* 1328)

Then, inserting crisp, befitting vernacular words/phrases into flawless English sentences.

(1) "and now Tai Bai leaning out of a window shouts, 'Hey, bhaenchaud! little sister-sleeper, where you running? What's true is true is true?" (*MC,* 320).

(2) "Where is this Sanaki Baba's camp? Where do all these sister-fucking pilgrims come from?" (*ASB,* 705)

The Coleridgean definition of good prose as "proper words in their proper place" is particularly significant in relation to the order of words and patterns of sentences commonly used by Indian creative writers in English. Indian novelists, like Rushdie and Seth, frequently break all rules of grammar to do creative writing in Indian English. Their path-finders, in different times, are three Irish writers—George Moore, George Bernard Shaw and James Joyce—who took liberty with the strict rules of Nesfield, coined new words and enriched the English language with vivacious prose. Peter Quennell reminds us that the best writing combines "a natural facility and an acquired difficulty."[4] Rushdie's writing contains this binary definition of style whereas Seth's contains the first half, i.e., "a natural facility." Rushdie, like Joyce, at first, opts for "acquired difficulty" but he would, like Joyce, achieve natural facility, in course of time. It means that Rushdie is a difficult writer but he holds the future. On the other hand, Seth, at first reading, is easily communicative but its communication would lose lustre as time passes. To put figuratively, *A Suitable Boy* is the Victoria Memorial of Calcutta and *Midnight's Children* is the Tajmahal, itself.

NOTES

1. Dilip Fernandez, "Such Angst, Loneliness, Rootlessness," *Gentleman,* February 1984, p. 103.
2. Devindra Kohli, "A Tragic Love Affair? The Contemporary Indian-English Literary Scene," *Aspects of Commonwealth Literature,* Vol. I (Oct. 1988-June 1989).
3. Vikram Seth in *The Telegraph Magazine,* 21 February 1993, p. 9.
4. *The Sign of the Fish* (New York: Viking, 1960), p. 88.

Bibliography

Primary Sources

Fiction

The Golden Gate. London: Faber and Faber, 1986. First ever modern novel in verse (593 sonnets written in iambic tetrameter). It is about a young man in the throes of a personal crisis who advertises for a girlfriend.
A Suitable Boy. New Delhi: Viking (Penguin India), 1993.

Tales

Beastly Tales from Here and There. New Delhi: Viking (Penguin India), 1992. A collection of 10 stories—two from India, two from China, two from Greece, two from the Ukraine and two "from the land of gup."

Poetry

Mappings. Calcutta: Writers Workshop.
The Humble Administrator's Garden. Carcacet, 1985.
All You Who Sleep Tonight. New Delhi: Viking (Penguin India), 1990.

Translation

Three Chinese Poets. New Delhi: Viking (Penguin India).

Travel Book

From Heaven Lake, Travels through Sinkiang and Tibet. London: Chatto and Windus, 1983.

Interviews

An Interview with Seema Paul. Calcutta: *The Telegraph Magazine*, 21 February 1993.
An Interview with Amit Roy. Calcutta: *The Telegraph*, 29 August 1992.

Secondary Sources

Campbell, Caryl. *A Suitable Boy*: Review, *In-between: Essays and Studies in Literary Criticism*, IV (March 1995), pp. 77-80.
Chaudhuri, Nirad C. *The Autobiography of an Unknown Indian*. Bombay: Jaico, 1969 (Third Impression).
_____. *Thy Hand, Great Anarch*. London: Chatto and Windus, 1987.
_____. *The Continent of Circe*. Bombay: Jaico.

Bibliography

_____. "British Rule is Dead, Long Live British Rule." Calcutta: *The Statesman* (Festivals), 1994.
Connolly, Cyril. *The Condemned Playground.* London: The Hogarth Press, 1985.
Dickens, Charles. *Martin Chuzzlewit.* Oxford: O.U.P.
Fernandez, Dilip. "Such Angst, Loneliness, Rootlessness." *Gentleman,* February 1984.
Gopal, Sarvepalli. London: *Encounter,* July/August 1989.
Greene, Graham. *The Honorary Consul.* New York: Pocket Books.
Kanga, Firdaus. "The Leaden Echo," *Poetry Review,* Spring 1993, Vol. 83, No. 1.
Kohli, Devindra. "A Tragic Love Affair? The Contemporary Indian-English Literary Scene" in *Aspects of Commonwealth Literature,* Vol. I (Oct. 1988-June 1989).
Lohia, Ram Manohar. *Interval during Politics.* Bombay: Sindhu.
Leavis, F.R. and Q.D. Leavis. *Dickens the Novelist.* Harmondsworth: Penguin, 1972.
Laslett, Peter. *The World We have Lost.* London: Methuen, 1985.
Limaye, Madhu. "Jawaharlal Nehru and Probity in Public Life." Calcutta: *The Statesman* (Festivals), 1994.
Mahadevan, T.K. *Ideas and Variations.* New Delhi: Mittal, 1988.
Myers, David. "Vikram Seth's Epic Renunciation of the Passions: Deconstructing Moral Codes in *A Suitable Boy,*" *Indian Literature Today,* ed. R.K. Dhawan (New Delhi: Prestige, 1994), pp.79-102.
Naik, M.K. *A History of Indian English Literature.* New Delhi: Sahitya Akademi, 1992 (rep.).
Panikkar, K.N. *Culture and Consciousness in Modern India.* New Delhi: People's Publishing House, 1990.
Prior, Moody E. *The Drama of Power: Studies in Shakespeare's History Plays.* Evanston, 1973.
Quennell, Peter. *The Sign of the Fish.* New York: Viking, 1960.
Radhakrishnan, S. *Vision of India.* New Delhi: Indian Council for Cultural Relations, 1988 (rep.).
Sarkar, Jadunath. *India through the Ages.* New Delhi: Sangam, 1979.
Schoenbaum, S. 'Richard II and the Realities of Power' in *Shakespeare Survey* (28), 1975.
Sengupta, S.C. *Swami Vivekananda and Indian Nationalism.* Calcutta: Sahitya Samsad, 1984.
L.K. Sharma, "Why *A Suitable Boy* was found unsuitable for Booker," *Times of India,* 27 Sept. 1993.
Tharoor, Shashi. "Writer at Work." *Gentleman,* 1990.
Walsh, William. *The Use of Imagination.* Harmondsworth: Penguin, 1966.

Index

Abbas, Khwaja Ahmad 32
Achebe, Chinua 78
Addison, Joseph 63
All about H. Hatterr 74
Ambedkar, B.R. 24
Anand, M.R. 32, 70, 73-78, 91, 92
And Gazelles Leaping 74
Atom and the Serpent 28
Aurobindo, Sri 51, 52, 54, 64, 68, 72
Austen, Jane 11, 12, 13, 24n, 70
Autobiography of an Unknown Indian, The 33-34, 60n, 86n
Azad, Abul Kalam 32

Bachchan, Harivansh Rai 32
Bend in the Ganges, A 74
Bhattacharya, Bhabani 32, 74
Bose, S.C. 32, 55, 60

"Chameleon," The 57
Chand, Prem 34
Chandra, Bankim 53, 63, 81
Chandra, Sarat 34
Chatterjee, Upamanyu 7, 8, 9, 10, 11, 74
Chaudhuri, Nirad C. 11, 33, 48n, 52-53, 61n, 79-81, 86n
Chekhov, Anton 57
Circle of Reason, The 10
Continent of Circe, The 24n

Dark Dancer, The 74, 76
Days of the Turban, The 10-11
Desai, Anita 74-75, 92
Desani, G.V. 74
Deshpande, Shashi 74
Dickens, Charles 7, 9, 11, 12, 13, 14, 24n, 62
Dr. Zhivago 24
Dumas, Alexander 62
Dutta, Michael Madhusudan 72

Eliot, George 63, 65, 70, 87
Eliot, T.S. 87, 89, 91
English, August 8, 10

Fielding, Henry 62
Forster, E.M. 13, 14, 16, 24, 63, 72

Gandhi, Indira 87, 88
Gandhi, M.K. 20, 31, 37, 48n, 55, 60, 72-74, 86n, 87
Gandhi, Rajiv 48n
Ghalib, Mirza 83, 84
Ghosh, Amitav 9, 10, 11, 74
Ghosh, Sudhindra Nath 74
Great Indian Novel, The 10
Greene, Graham 11, 18, 19, 24n

Hardy, Thomas 13
Heart of Midlothian, The 62
Henry Ermond 62, 63
Honorary Consul, The 18, 24n
Howards End 16, 69

Identity Card 8
Inqilab 32
Iqbal, Mohd. 32, 90

James, Henry 7, 87
Jigar 32
Joyce, James 21, 68, 69, 72, 85-87, 93

Kalidas 50, 61n
Kanga, Firdaus 27, 30n
Kanthapura 70, 77
Keshavasut 32
Kidwai, Rafi Ahmed 17, 35, 36, 42, 43, 44, 91
Kim 72
Kipling, Rudyard 72
Kripalani, Acharya 17, 32, 35-37, 40

Lawrence, D.H. 16, 24n
Limaye, Madhu 42, 48n
Lohia, Ram Manohar 91

Madhaviah, A. 72
Mahabharata, The 7, 10
Malgonkar, Manohar 74
Mardhekar 32
Martin Chuzzlewit 7, 13, 14, 23, 24
Maugham, Somerset 53
Middlemarch 7, 63, 65
Midnight's Children 29, 70, 74, 77, 87, 88, 90-93
Mir, Mir Taqi 83
Mookaji's Visions 70
Moore, George 85, 93
Mukherjee, Bharati 7
Mukherjee, Hiren 35, 38
Murthy, Anantha 70

Naidu, Sarojini 32, 72
Nandakumar, Prema 28, 30n
Narayan, J.P. 91
Narayan, R.K. 7, 11, 12, 32, 70, 73, 78, 86n, 91
Nehru, J.L. 9, 11, 17, 21, 26, 27, 30n, 32-37, 39-41, 43, 45, 46, 64-69, 71, 73, 78, 87, 88, 91, 92
Nirala, Suryakant 32

Old Men at the Zoo, The 56

Panchatantra 70
Pant, Govind Vallabh 17, 37
Passage to India, A 72

Patel, Vallabhbhai 32, 33. 37, 45
Parvez, Salahuddin 8
Pilgrim's Progress 53
Pillai, T. Ramakrishna 72
Prasad, Rajendra 32, 37, 47n
Pride and Prejudice 12-13, 24n, 65

Raag Darbari 11, 24n
Radhakrishnan, S. 71
Raghuvamsam 61
Rajagopalachari, C. 32, 38, 45
Rajan, B. 74, 78
Rao, Raja 32, 70, 73-74, 76, 77, 91
Rich Like Us 24
Road, The 76, 77
Roy, Raja Rammohan 50, 51, 61
Rushdie, Salman 70, 74, 75, 77, 86, 88-93

Sahgal, Nayantara 8, 9, 11, 18-21
Samskara 70
Scott, Walter 62
Shadow Lines, The 10
Shame 74, 87, 89-92
Sharma, Partap 7, 9, 10-11
Shukla, S lal 11, 23, 24
Sibal, Nina 9, 10, 11
Singh, Khushwant 74, 75, 77, 78, 92
So Many Hungers 74
Story of the Stone, The 70

Tagore, R.N. 35, 51, 52, 55, 56, 64, 90
Tale of Two Cities, A 62-63
Tandon, Purusuttomdas 32, 65, 91
Thackeray, W.M. 53, 62, 63, 65
Tharoor, Shashi 9, 10, 17
This Time of Morning 18
Three Musketeers, The 62
Tolstoy, Leo 7, 53, 56, 60, 61, 63, 70
Tom Jones 62
Train to Pakistan 74, 77
Twilight in Delhi 83
Two Leaves and a Bud 70

Ulysses 86
Untouchable 70

Vallathol 32
Vanity Fair 65
Venkataramani, K.S. 32, 73
Verma, Mahadevi 32
Vivekananda, Swami 61n

War and Peace 24, 30, 53, 56, 60, 63, 65
Wilson, Angus 56

Yatra 10